Shridath Ramphal

The Commonwealth and the World

Shridath Ramphal

The Commonwealth and the World

ESSAYS IN HONOUR OF HIS 80th BIRTHDAY

Edited by Richard Bourne

HANSIB

Published by Hansib Publications in 2008
London & Hertfordshire

Hansib Publications Limited
P.O. Box 226, Hertford, Hertfordshire, SG14 3WY, United Kingdom

Email: info@hansib-books.com
Website: www.hansib-books.com

A catalogue record of this book is
available from the British Library

ISBN 978-1-906190-20-0

© The Ramphal Centre, UK

Cover design by Graphic Resolutions, Hertfordshire

Printed and bound in the UK

For Sonny

David Dabydeen

The lumps of gold which Raleigh grasped
For, digging up mountains, trawling
Lakes, losing countless men, a beloved
Son, his own sanity and head.
His maps were confused, directionless.
Gold slipped from his grasp
Like breath. He brought back only
News of the dead.

Three centuries and more since he sighted land.
Another sea crossing, another stranger
Came to El Dorado's shore,
From India, shovel, cutlass in hand,
Cleared space in the canefield, a manger
For his wife. On the seventh day his work
Was done. The child she bore:
Shridath, pathway to a golden sun.

— ∞ —

Professor David Dabydeen, born in Guyana, won the Commonwealth Poetry Prize in 1984 and holds a chair in the Centre for Translation and Comparative Cultural Studies at Warwick University, of which Sonny Ramphal was Chancellor from 1989 to 2002.

Contents

Editorial Note and Acknowledgements

It has been a privilege to edit this collection. In the absence of any full-length biography of Shridath "Sonny" Ramphal, and with the inclusion of material and commentary which will be new to most readers, I believe that this is not just a tribute to a major international personality on his 80th birthday, but a lasting contribution to contemporary history.

As editor I have not sought to harmonise the different perspectives of our authors, to all of whom I owe deepest thanks. My concern has been with readability and the checking of facts. All the authors are extremely busy people. They have responded generously and speedily. Publication of this book is one of a number of celebrations for Sonny Ramphal, organised by a London committee chaired by Mrs Patsy Robertson, which has also promoted the Ramphal Centre, and a special lecture on his 80th birthday in October, 2008.

I would therefore like to acknowledge with thanks: each of our authors, in alphabetical order – Guy Arnold, Vincent Cable, Derek Ingram, Moni Malhoutra, James Manor, Rex Nettleford, Anthony Payne, Bishnodat Persaud, S K Rao, Patsy Robertson, Sir Ronald Sanders, Kaye Whiteman; those who have supplied and given permission for the reproduction of pictures – Lady Susan Sanders and the Ramphal family, the Commonwealth Secretariat (with thanks to Kevin Nellies), the Press Association and Oxford Mail; and particularly our publisher – Arif Ali of Hansib, and his colleagues; and other members of the Ramphal Centre Committee for their advice and encouragement. Finally I should like to thank my wife Juliet, who has provided invaluable IT assistance.

Richard Bourne

List of illustrations

Front: Shridath Ramphal on a Marlborough House staircase
Back: A recent portrait
Photo sections:
- The young "Sonny" Ramphal growing up in Guyana
- With his father, "J I" in British Guiana.
- British Guiana's youngest "Silk"
- Chancellor of Warwick University, with his mother, Grace
- Shridath and Lady Ramphal, with their grandchildren
- In celebratory mood after Zimbabwe's independence election
- The anti-apartheid struggle
- The Commonwealth Eminent Persons Group
- With Cuba's Revolutionary leader, Fidel Castro
- Nelson Mandela's first visit to London
- Presenting President Mandela with an honorary degree at Warwick
- At the 1966 Commonwealth Heads of Government Meeting
- A meeting of Commonwealth Caribbean Attorneys-General
- Agreement to establish the Caribbean Community and Common Market (CARICOM)
- Ramphal and West Indian Cricket hero, Clive Lloyd
- The 'new' Secretary-General conferring with his predecessor
- Escorting the Queen
- Ramphal's first Heads of Government Meeting as Secretary-General
- With Prime Minister Pierre Trudeau of Canada
- Photograph of Prime Minister Margaret Thatcher inscribed to "Sonny"
- With Prime Minister Indira Gandhi
- Five Commonwealth Heads of Government in a Melbourne garden
- With President Kaunda and Prime Ministers Trudeau and Ratu Mara
- At the annual Blenheim Palace cricket match
- With the Duke of Edinburgh
- At the UN Security Council in 1975
- With Willy Brandt
- With Lord Scarman

Introduction

— ∞ —

Richard Bourne

— ∞ —

"We must never underestimate the influence of the eloquent, reflective and disinterested mind. We should not underestimate Mr Ramphal" – **Barbara Ward, 1979**

"He is one of those men who have become famous because, in their fight for human justice, they have chosen the entire world as their theatre" – **Nelson Mandela, 1990**

Shridath Ramphal, better known by his boyhood name Sonny, grew up in Guyana in the colonial era to become the leading spokesman of the free, independent, developing world in the last quarter of the 20th century. He engaged with great issues – the removal of racism from southern Africa, the need for fairer trade and real socioeconomic development for the four-fifths of people who live in poverty, the challenge of a depleting environment, the overriding requirement for a generous cooperation between nations.

He made the case for change. His vantage point was not one of power in the traditional sense, but he used the power of ideas and the power of persuasion. For an unequalled stint of 15 years, from 1975 to 1990, he was Secretary-General of the Commonwealth of Nations. He served on a succession of international commissions, led by Willy Brandt, Gro-Harlem Brundtland, and Olof Palme. The essays which follow, in honour of his 80th birthday in late 2008, provide snapshots of a remarkable career. They cannot do justice to everything he did, or the lives he touched with his leadership.

— ∞ —

Richard Bourne, Senior Research Fellow at the Institute of Commonwealth Studies, is secretary to the Ramphal Centre Committee and was first Head of the Commonwealth Policy Studies Unit (1998-2005) and first Director of the Commonwealth Human Rights Initiative (1990-1992)

He was born in Berbice, in what was then British Guiana, on 3 October, 1928, to James and Grace Ramphal. His great-grandmother had come to the country as an indentured worker in the previous century from Bihar, a poor Indian state. She was one of the large number of workers recruited from the subcontinent by sugar planters, who wanted to replace African slave labour on their plantations after emancipation. She was a widow of great courage, arriving in Georgetown in 1881 after a four month voyage from Calcutta, with a nine year old son, all set to take on a third five-year set of indentures. The nine year old boy, called Daniel, was himself indentured at that age and only technically released from his indentures in 1932.

Nearly all Indians were Hindus or Muslims. But Daniel Ramphal went to a mission school run by the Canadian Presbyterian Church. He became a Christian and trained as a teacher. His son James, known as Jimmy, also taught, and came to run the most prestigious private secondary school in the colony. Jimmy's bright son, Shridath Surendranath, went from Georgetown to London in 1947 to train for the law. He was called to the Bar at Gray's Inn in 1951 – the year he married Lois King – and the following year he got his Master's degree in law at King's College, London, earning a distinction.

At this stage of his career there was little, apart from his obvious intelligence, which might have suggested anything other than a lifetime to be spent in the law. In London he joined Dingle Foot's chamber of barristers and he returned to Georgetown, becoming Crown Counsel and Assistant Attorney-General at the tender age of 25. With the larger Caribbean colonies on the verge of independence he was appointed as Solicitor-General in 1959.

But he then took a course which showed independence of mind. He threw in his lot with the ill-fated Federation of the West Indies, serving as its Assistant Attorney-General, based in Trinidad, from 1961-2. The Federation was designed to bring together all the Caribbean islands and territories; it would take advantage of their common political and cultural heritage, but also offset their relative smallness and weakness as individual jurisdictions.

Most of the South Asian community in Guyana was opposed to the Federation, and Guyana decided to stay out. But Sonny's father, Jimmy Ramphal, who was on the Legislative Council of the colony from 1954-7, was an enthusiast for the Federation. The continuing friction between Afro-Guyanese and the South Asian community, known as East Indians, had led to a political split between their leaders in 1955, Forbes Burnham and Cheddi Jagan respectively.

Ramphal was engaged in drafting a constitution for the Federation, due to become independent in 1962, when it suddenly collapsed. A No vote in a referendum in Jamaica was the killer blow. Reflecting on this much later, in a speech in Nigeria in 1976, Sonny concluded that the participants in the Caribbean were not sufficiently willing to put the interests of the Federation ahead of their insular concerns. It was perhaps a significant lesson in the fragility of international cooperation, and the importance of maintaining both public and elite support – a lesson he never forgot.

Guyana continued its controversial progress towards independence, with communal conflict, and United States and United Kingdom machinations to prevent the "communist" Cheddi Jagan from taking power. In 1965 Forbes Burnham became premier of a coalition government; the following year, in May, Guyana was independent. Like nearly all former colonies it joined the Commonwealth, which had set up its multilateral Secretariat in London the previous year. Sonny accepted Burnham's invitation to become Attorney-General. He did not, however, become a member of Burnham's largely Afro-Guyanese party, the People's National Congress.

The year after independence, Sonny became involved in foreign affairs as well as justice, and from 1973-5 he held both these senior portfolios. It was at this time that his international reputation was built. Guyana, and the other newly-independent Caribbean countries, faced two enormous challenges. The first was to rescue their regional identity and interests from the setback of the defeat of Federation. The second was harder still: it was to protect the export trade of developing countries after the United Kingdom joined the European Community in January 1973.

Sonny worked simultaneously on these two problems, making significant alliances and friendships in the process. At the Treaty of Chaguaramas, in May 1973, the Caribbean states agreed to build a Caribbean Community, going beyond the regional free trade area – inspired by Guyana – which already existed. Appropriately, the CARICOM secretariat was to be sited in Georgetown.

The issue with the European Community affected former British colonies in Africa, Caribbean and the Pacific. All would lose their preferential access to the UK market unless something fresh was negotiated. Caribbean exports of sugar, bananas, and citrus were vulnerable. By July 1973, at the first meeting of ministers of ACP countries, Sonny spoke on behalf of the Caribbean. He pointed out that, in a region where unemployment ran from 15-25 per cent, it was ridiculous to talk of the reciprocal opening of markets.

After 19 months of arduous talks, when ACP states rejected the three different commercial arrangements proposed by the Community under its protocol 22 of the Treaty of Accession, a deal was signed at Lomé in Togo. The countries concerned had got better market access in Europe than they had had in the UK alone, as well as other benefits from what was described as development cooperation. It was generally recognised that the Foreign Minister of Guyana had played a crucial role in building an alliance between diverse governments, and deploying a common case.

The Lomé Convention – the first of many EC/ACP agreements – was signed in February 1975. By this time Sonny was preparing to take up the assignment for which he is best known, as Commonwealth Secretary-General. The Caribbean and ACP work he had done had given him a strong support base; Canada was a key backer; Indira Gandhi, when he visited her in New Delhi, told him it was important that the Commonwealth should become more effective.

The Commonwealth Secretariat, set up by Arnold Smith, a Canadian, was only a decade old as a multilateral institution. It had weathered the Nigerian civil war, a war between its two largest members, India and Pakistan, and a major row when the UK had wanted to sell arms to white South Africa in 1971. Rhodesia's "unilateral declaration of independence" was still unresolved, with a burgeoning bush war. Non-aligned and developing member states were looking for a new lead. Sonny was only 46 when he became Secretary-General, younger than nearly all the presidents and prime ministers with whom he would be working.

Sonny made it clear from the start that he wanted the Commonwealth to take a key role in development, to promote the New International Economic Order, and to try and offset western control of information and global capital. The Yom Kippur war, and the OPEC oil price rises had challenged western complacency, although it had also threatened the economies of non-oil developing states. In a sequence of speeches and writings, in his management of meetings of Commonwealth Heads over the 15 years he was Secretary-General, and in his promotion of Commonwealth expert groups on developmental issues, Sonny tried to push the agenda forward.

The campaign for one-man-one-vote in Rhodesia, and the Commonwealth struggle to end apartheid in South Africa, won many headlines, as well as criticism from reactionaries. Idi Amin's attempt to hijack the London summit of 1977 by threatening to come to it led to the first Commonwealth statement for human rights and, at Gleneagles in Scotland, a sporting boycott of the apartheid regime was agreed.

In spite of Margaret Thatcher's election win for the Conservatives in the UK in 1979, the Lusaka summit that year opened the way to a full settlement for Zimbabwe. Sonny deftly turned around the British Government's initial support for Bishop Abel Muzorewa; a Commonwealth election observer group in 1980 watched as guerrillas moved into designated camps, and voters chose a government led by Robert Mugabe.

Southern Africa remained a driving concern for Sonny, as internal opposition to the apartheid regime grew, and Pretoria took over sponsorship of Renamo guerrillas in neighbouring Mozambique to fight the ruling Frelimo government. A liberation war in Namibia, the League of Nations mandate territory which South Africa had tried to annexe, became more serious in the 1980s, with South African incursions into Angola.

Sonny was central to the diplomatic effort, not only because he was trusted by the front line African states; India, for instance, had never had official relations with South Africa since 1947, due to revulsion at apartheid. Although the British Government of Margaret Thatcher was grateful for Commonwealth support when Argentina invaded the Falklands in 1982, the Secretary-General clashed with her repeatedly over South Africa.

The contest over how best to move South Africa to full, multiracial democracy came to a head at a disputatious Commonwealth summit in the Bahamas in 1985, which agreed limited sanctions against the white regime, and an Eminent Persons Group (EPG) to visit South Africa. Sonny had managed to weld the diverse approaches of leaders in Nassau into a compromise effort to produce a negotiated end to apartheid. The EPG was jointly led by former Nigerian president Olusegun Obasanjo, and former Australian prime minister, Malcolm Fraser.

The group met the imprisoned Nelson Mandela three times, and seemed to make progress with the white politicians; it produced a "negotiating concept" which would have ended the banning of the African National Congress, and led to a truce in military actions. But the mission was aborted when the securocrats in the Pretoria regime bombed three neighbouring Commonwealth states. The account of the mission became a best-seller.

Sonny's last five years as Secretary-General, until 1990, saw a continued struggle to end apartheid. But, although much detailed work still had to be done, he had the satisfaction of knowing that the struggle was moving into its final phase, signalled by the fall of the Berlin wall in 1989, Mandela's release from prison in February 1990, and Namibia's independence the following month. Much of the ideology of the apartheid regime had depended on its purported opposition to a "communist threat", which had plainly evaporated.

A second area in which Sonny gave intellectual leadership lay in trade and development, and the need to strengthen multilateralism. He recognised that one of the key assets of the Commonwealth was its brainpower, allied to its diversity. He used the technique of the expert group, bringing together persons from different countries and backgrounds to make recommendations to governments.

In the decade from 1977-87 alone he sponsored eleven expert groups, with a heavy emphasis on development and international economic issues. In 1977 his Caribbean friend Allister McIntyre chaired a study on the New International Economic Order; Lord Harold Lever, a close associate of the former British prime minister, Harold Wilson, chaired a study on international debt which prefigured campaigns for debt write-off over the next two decades; an expert group on the vulnerability of small states, which reported in 1985, launched a new awareness of this issue; and in 1987 Peter Kirby chaired a group on the future of jobs for young people.

Sonny was also ahead of his time in giving attention to environmental issues. He was pleased in 1989 when President Hoyte of Guyana, at the Kuala Lumpur summit, offered a million acres of rainforest for the pioneering Iwokrama programme, for conservation and sustainable development.

However, much of this development campaigning was uphill work. Sonny's convinced multilateralism had led him to join Willy Brandt, the former West German Chancellor, Edward Heath, the former British Prime Minister, and other well-known figures in an independent commission on international development issues (1977-83). Non-governmental organisations in the North, and governments in the South, hoped that it could break the logjam in trade and aid issues. Optimists thought that a special international summit in Cancun in Mexico, in October 1981, would lead to a breakthrough.

Instead it demonstrated a new conservative axis, led by President Reagan and Prime Minister Thatcher. They not only wanted to block transfers of resources to the governments of poor countries, and the opening of rich countries' markets. They sought to promote monetarism, liberal economics, and a reconstructed world order based on private enterprise. They were suspicious not only of socialism and state-based development, but of multilateralism itself.

During most of Sonny's time in the public eye, he was having to argue a multilateral case against tough and determined opposition. He once remarked that in the Commonwealth there is no centre and no periphery; he also knew that Commonwealth action on its own is insufficient – "the Commonwealth cannot negotiate for the world, but it can help the world to negotiate." He was a confirmed and dedicated internationalist.

He therefore threw himself not only into the Brandt Commission, providing it with invaluable back-up from professionals at the Commonwealth Secretariat. He took part in a range of related activities, including the Palme commission on disarmament and security issues (1980-82), the Brundtland commission on environment and development (1984-87), and the South Commission (1987-90). From 1984-7 he chaired the UN committee on development planning. Even after leaving the Commonwealth Secretariat he was still playing this role – in the Carnegie commission on preventing deadly conflict (1994-98) and as co-chair of the commission on global governance (1992-2000).

These efforts helped to change global thinking. Sometimes the practical impacts came years later. For example the Brundtland commission gave birth to the Earth Summit in Rio de Janeiro in 1992, where Sonny was a special adviser to the UN Secretary-General and wrote the conference book, "Our Country, the Planet". That in itself led on to the Agenda 21, where local communities take environmental action, and to the Kyoto Protocol, by which governments seek to reduce global warming. Ramphal was an ideas man who recognised that, in the international arena, change comes slowly and most things require a long haul.

Sonny was also pivotal to the survival and development of the Commonwealth. At the end of the sixties and in the early seventies, with countries like Nigeria and Tanzania threatening to leave in protest at British policy in southern Africa, and the antics of Idi Amin damaging its claims to principle, many forecast that it would split and die. It was after all a club which had emerged from the British Empire, in which the UK, Canada and Australia were paying 70 per cent of its Secretariat's income.

What Sonny did was to show that, while having regard to the concerns of the UK and the former dominions, he would reflect the views of the membership as a whole. The paymasters would not call the tune. Further, there were many things that the Commonwealth needed to do, not all of them political.

For instance, Sonny commissioned a team led by Asa Briggs to conduct a study of what distance learning could do for the Commonwealth. Increased fees in old Commonwealth countries had reduced student mobility, and the opportunities of students from smaller and poorer states. Following this study a Commonwealth of Learning was set up in Vancouver, to give a fillip to distance education and Open Universities round the Commonwealth. Its latest manifestation is a virtual university for small states with open access materials, using internet technology.

The vitality of the Commonwealth in his era attracted and retained many gifted individuals for its Secretariat. Among them were Chief Emeka Anyaoku, the long-serving Deputy Secretary-General (Political) from Nigeria, and Moni Malhoutra from India, who subsequently returned to New Delhi to direct the Rajiv Gandhi Foundation. Chief Anyaoku had briefly been Foreign Minister of his country, and it was said during Sonny's term that permanent secretaries at home would happily move to London to take up more junior positions in the Commonwealth Secretariat, for the sheer excitement of being part of it.

This introduction can merely skim the surface of a period in Commonwealth history of constant challenge, with a coup in Nigeria, a US invasion of Grenada, and growing warfare in southern Africa. Sonny, like all Secretaries-General, had to spend much of each year away from his Secretariat's historic London home in Marlborough House, crossing time zones, and taking advantage of his friendship with leaders of different political complexions to pursue quiet diplomacy.

Twice reelected as Secretary-General, Sonny's third term at Marlborough House came to an end in mid-1990. The Prime Minister of Malaysia took the election of his successor as first business at the Kuala Lumpur summit the previous year, where Chief Anyaoku comfortably beat Malcolm Fraser, the former Australian prime minister.

Sonny left the Commonwealth Secretariat as a still youthful 61. Many organisations and individuals were begging him for help. He was Chancellor of the universities of Guyana and Warwick, and the

University of the West Indies. He chaired the West Indian Commission, which charted a future for the region in the 21st century, and he set up the regional negotiating machinery which sought a unified Caribbean trading response to the European Community, the United States and the World Trade Organisation.

He acted as a facilitator in the long-running Belize-Guatemala boundary dispute, which had not entirely been resolved with international recognition of Belizean independence. His life-long multilateralism was displayed again when he co-chaired with the Prime Minister of Sweden a commission on global governance, from 1992-2000. Its report, "Our Global Neighbourhood", reflected much of his vision.

He was showered with honours, asked to deliver addresses and lectures around the world, and received a second knighthood from the Queen, as a tribute to his work for the Commonwealth. Everywhere people wanted a piece of his reflective wisdom, and to hear again his mellifluous and persuasive Guyanese voice. At a time when speech-making is not always appreciated, and images and abbreviated text messages pass for communication, the humane Ramphal vision seems evergreen.

Two small examples of his eloquence, from 1987, will suffice. Ramphal worked closely with both Indira Gandhi and her son Rajiv, both prime ministers who were murdered by extremists. On 19 January 1987, giving the Indira Gandhi memorial lecture in New Delhi, he said:

> "None of us anywhere, in the First World or the Third, can speak of peace but listen only to the drums of war. We cannot yearn for peace, but live by an ethos of power. We cannot pray for peace, but nurture hate and prejudice and selfishness in our hearts. The peace of the world comes from within each and every one of the people who inhabit it. For every one of us, in however small a measure, peace is in our keeping."

Sonny's speeches were carefully researched, and mixed mischievous humour with enlightenment. Later the same year he was giving a lecture at the Royal Society of Arts in London and said:

"Mahatma Gandhi was once asked what he thought of western civilisation. He reflected for a while and then answered cautiously, 'I think it would be a good idea.'"

And Sonny isn't finished yet. In 2007, on behalf of Guyana, he led a team of eminent international lawyers to success in a marathon maritime boundary arbitration – with Suriname – under the UN Convention on the Law of the Sea. This UN Convention had, more than 30 years earlier, been initiated by a Commonwealth member, Malta, and lawyers working for different Commonwealth states had played a crucial role in its negotiation.

The award, in favour of Guyana, was delivered on the eve of Sonny's 79th birthday. He hailed it as "a victory for the rule of law."

The collection of essays which follows, by people who worked with him or who followed his career closely, reflects different viewpoints, provides some context, and can highlight only some of his achievements. It is designed to throw light on the career of an energetic international statesman, who spent crucial years with a poorly-understood network, the Commonwealth. He and his collaborators have had a significant influence on the world we know now. It is hard to believe that he can be 80. Happy birthday Sonny!

Shridath Ramphal: personal reflections

— ∞ —

Me and my boss: the Sonny experience

Moni Malhoutra

— ∞ —

"What will you have for breakfast tomorrow morning?" Sonny asks me. I am puzzled by the question.

We are in New York in 1975 for the United Nations General Assembly. We are booked to stay at the Plaza Hotel on Central Park South, but walk out in protest when the hotel asks to take an imprint of our credit cards. The practice is relatively new and we are not familiar with it. We think it implies distrust of us personally. With great difficulty, we then manage to find accommodation in an apartment hotel near the United Nations.

"I will decide tomorrow when I go to the corner restaurant," I reply. "But I would like to cook breakfast for you in my apartment. I am asking you now so that I can go out to buy the necessary provisions."

I am taken aback. Sonny has been Secretary-General for about three months and has inducted me into the Secretary-General's office. In India, where I belong, strict codes of hierarchy prevail. It is unthinkable for a superior to do such a thing. "I love cooking", Sonny adds. "Just tell me what you would like to eat."

I arrive at Sonny's apartment the next morning to find the table already laid. I feel a little awkward sitting and watching him cook my breakfast. Orange juice, waffles, scrambled eggs and bacon, hot buttered toast and coffee follow in quick succession. It does not even

— ∞ —

Moni Malhoutra was Assistant Secretary-General for the Commonwealth,1982 - 1993, and subsequently Secretary-General of the Rajiv Gandhi Foundation, New Delhi, 2001- 2007.

occur to me to offer to help with the washing up. I am, after all, from India, where we leave such tasks to others.

I narrate the story to a friend. "All that I can say", he replies, "is that your boss is working too hard to secure your loyalty". It is the start of a very close working relationship and an enduring personal friendship.

I first met Sonny in 1973 when he had come to call on Indira Gandhi with whom I worked. He looked younger than his years, almost boyish, with his face flushed by Delhi's intense summer heat. We chatted amiably in the anteroom, waiting to go in. Indira Gandhi was then at the height of her power. Overseas visitors sometimes felt a little intimidated in her presence. One African High Commissioner, calling on her for the first time, sat in complete silence, unable to utter a word. Not Sonny. All his Caribbean charm was in full flow and the rapport between him and Mrs. Gandhi was very evident. He spoke to her about the situation in Guyana and of the Non-Aligned Foreign Ministers' Meeting of which he was host. He described the Amerindian-style structure of the Conference venue which appealed greatly to her fine aesthetic sensibilities. He finally broached his intention of standing for election as Secretary-General of the Commonwealth and hoped India would support him.

Mrs. Gandhi was taken aback. "You are doing such a fine job as Foreign Minister. Why do you want to move to the Commonwealth position? It will be a loss for all of us."

Sonny explained his reasons. The Commonwealth offered a unique North-South platform. If it could be helped to become more outward-looking, it could be harnessed to stimulate consensus on a number of divisive international issues, at the same time advancing the interests of developing countries on many fronts.

I could see that Mrs. Gandhi remained sceptical. Her own experience of the Commonwealth did not suggest to her that Sonny's hopes were feasible. She nevertheless promised India's support. "I hope you will shake up the Commonwealth", she said smilingly.

Arnold Smith, the first Secretary-General, was a Canadian diplomat. He had been preoccupied with the task of establishing the

Commonwealth Secretariat from scratch, negotiating its status and privileges, gradually expanding its activities in the face of considerable opposition, and building up the Commonwealth Fund for Technical Cooperation.

Sonny Ramphal brought a new set of talents to Marlborough House, which made working with him exciting. He was much more articulate and had a fine way with words. Not without reason, he was often described as 'His Eloquence' rather than 'His Excellency'. His powers of persuasion were impressive, and he could stand his ground in any discussion. His mastery of the facts was always thorough. He had charm and humour, and could jolly things along when jolliness was needed. He was media savvy, even if on occasion a trifle wordy. He was a skilled negotiator, with a sharp legal mind. He also knew how to mobilise his assets in pursuit of an important objective. During the Retreat at the Nassau Commonwealth Heads of Government Meeting in 1985, the issue of sanctions against South Africa dominated the proceedings and threatened to split the Commonwealth. How was Mrs. Thatcher to be persuaded? Who would best be able to bell the cat? "We must enlist our three best-looking Prime Ministers to negotiate with Mrs. Thatcher", Sonny told me. They were Rajiv Gandhi of India, Brian Mulroney of Canada and Bob Hawke of Australia – a happy combination of good looks and political weight which Mrs. Thatcher would find difficult to ignore. He was political to his fingertips, quick in his grasp of political nuances and motivations and how to play on them to best effect. He was extremely well-tuned into world affairs, with a wide range of contacts and friendships with prominent political personalities. All these were qualities which he deployed with great effect. Working with him became a learning experience for all of us. His informality and camaraderie endeared him to everyone in Marlborough House, and many beyond it. He was that rare public figure from the developing world, a man without pomposity, stuffiness, or sense of self-importance.

Admirable personal qualities cannot, in themselves, be enough. Sonny Ramphal came to his job with a clear vision of what he wished to do. The Commonwealth is a curious entity among international organisations, neither fish nor fowl. What kind of role could it usefully play? All international organisations depend heavily on the quality of their leadership, and Sonny proved to be an exceptional leader. It was obvious from the start that he relished the transition from Guyana to London, and the wider opportunities which the Commonwealth offered. As Sonny put it, although the Commonwealth could not negotiate for the world, it could help the world to negotiate. It could do so because its diverse membership straddled all the major negotiating groups and made it a unique sample of the world community. The Commonwealth could also be a progenitor of ideas to promote international cooperation in new areas. His enthusiasm for the Commonwealth, and his belief in its capacity to influence events, were unflagging. Not all Commonwealth leaders were as starry-eyed: whether Indira Gandhi or Mahathir Mohammed, it was Sonny Ramphal who brought them around to an appreciation of the Commonwealth's worth. He was quick to visit every newly-elected Commonwealth Prime Minister to canvas his vision of the Commonwealth, answer questions, allay doubts, and build a personal relationship with each of them. In the face of British coolness to the association and the UK media's generally dismissive attitude, these proved to be countervailing assets of great value. A relationship of trust was built up which made possible the major achievements of his term of office.

I accompanied Sonny on many of his trips and sat in on many of his meetings, observing the skill with which he cultivated the Commonwealth's political leadership. With the exception of Mr Muldoon of New Zealand, he was received everywhere with warmth. Commonwealth leaders accorded him respect. They found their conversations with him stimulating. He always had something of interest to tell them about the world at large. He was full of ideas, planting seeds in their minds about how the Commonwealth could be made more effective, how regional cooperation could be strengthened, and how a variety of issues might usefully be dealt with.

In this he was assisted by the quality of staff he was able to attract to the Commonwealth Secretariat. Not all were high flyers, but enough of them were. Sonny resisted the notion that member countries should have staff quotas. The broad principle of adequate geographical representation was tempered by an emphasis on merit. Although a relatively small organisation, the Secretariat was high not only in quality, but in motivation under Ramphal's leadership. An effective Secretariat helped him to refine and develop his own ideas and to pursue them with vigour. There were Commonwealth Expert Groups on a range of issues, including a pioneering one on the issue of climate change. The Commonwealth was first in the field on this issue, thanks to Sonny.

Long before the concept became fashionable, Sonny made the Secretariat a "flat" organisation, with hierarchical barriers reduced to encourage a flow of ideas as well as to foster team spirit. He never pretended to any superior wisdom, kept an open mind and welcomed argument and counter-argument. He was generous in his praise for tasks well done, giving credit where credit was due. He was less good at pulling up those who didn't perform. At a personal level, he shied away from confrontation and was often unwilling, within the Secretariat, to bringing erring colleagues or staff into line. I'm still not sure whether this was out of innocence, weakness or misplaced tolerance. Paradoxically, he was not averse to confrontation on big matters, or taking the risks that such confrontation might entail. His disagreements with Margaret Thatcher and Lord Carrington are well publicised, but there were others as well with different political personalities on a variety of issues.

What mattered most was that he was always there to give us counsel and advice when we were out on difficult field missions as, for instance, during the Commonwealth Observer Group's work in Rhodesia and later, during the mission of the Commonwealth Eminent Persons' Group to South Africa.

One quality which we all admired and which stood the Commonwealth in good stead was his ability as a draftsman. His political skills and legal background made him a superb bridge-builder between different points of view. The Commonwealth drew heavily on this particular Ramphal skill. "You must always be ahead of the game," he told me, "by having a draft ready in your pocket to table at the right moment." It was this tactic which contributed greatly to the resolution of divisive issues at successive Heads of Government meetings. Ramphal's penmanship underlay the Gleneagles statement on the sporting boycott of South Africa; it was also the basis of the Lusaka Accord on Rhodesia, where Ramphal cobbled together common elements from the positions of Julius Nyerere, Kenneth Kaunda and Mrs Thatcher around which agreement might be possible. When the draft Accord was prematurely leaked by the Australians to the media, Sonny's intervention proved critical in ensuring that the Accord itself was not scuttled. Again at the Nassau CHOGM in 1985, I remember sitting with Sonny for hours and giving him such help as I could as he worked laboriously on drafting the Commonwealth Accord on Southern Africa. He confided to me that if Britain dissociated itself from it he would resign, as this would represent both a personal failure and a severe weakening of the Commonwealth's efforts to achieve a non-racial South Africa. Although Britain remained in the Commonwealth tent at Nassau on the issue of South Africa, it opted out at Vancouver in 1987 and Kuala Lumpur in 1989. By then, it was clear that any patchwork formula to keep Britain in would be at the cost of damaging the Commonwealth's credibility in the eyes of all the rest of its members, as well as internationally. In the event, the Commonwealth gained in confidence and cohesion, demonstrating a capacity to act without British participation.

Rhodesia's transition to majority rule and the struggle to end apartheid in South Africa were the two most testing issues of Ramphal's tenure of office.

Ramphal's skills in political management were much in evidence in the wake of the Lusaka Accord on Rhodesia. He was constantly on the phone to the Presidents of the Frontline States to ensure that the Patriotic Front – ZAPU and ZANU – did not boycott the Lancaster House Conference as they had threatened to do. Denied the status of an Observer at the conference, Sonny finessed his exclusion by convening regular meetings of the Commonwealth Committee on Southern Africa, both to be briefed on the progress of the conference and to find ways of overcoming difficulties and disagreements. He was also signalling that the Commonwealth was an important player itself and intended to remain so. Key Commonwealth leaders like Kenneth Kaunda, Michael Manley, Julius Nyerere and Malcolm Fraser came in at different stages and helped to forge the necessary compromises. Each kept in the closest touch with Sonny and consulted him in advance at every step. He was like a spider at the centre of a web. Equally important was his role in keeping Mugabe and Nkomo at the negotiating table, helping to allay their fears of British trickery and finding solutions to their objections. Although Lord Carrington was dismissive of Sonny's role and regarded him as a meddling hocus-pocus, he was in fact pivotal to the success of the conference. He proved to be a tireless behind-the-scenes mediator, shuttling between all the principal players. Ariston Chambati, one of Nkomo's aides, later said: "We nicknamed him 'the Mouse', because he scurried back and forth. When we had a difficult situation, Nkomo would say, 'Call the Mouse.' He was negotiating a settlement, very quietly passing on messages to both sides. His role was appreciated." Without Sonny's interposition, the deadlock over land compensation would not have been broken, there would have been no collective Commonwealth Observer Group or Commonwealth Monitoring Force or revised ceasefire terms: without these components, the Patriotic Front would have returned to the bush to resume the war. The Commonwealth's central role in ensuring Rhodesia's peaceful transition to majority rule owed much to Sonny Ramphal's energy and ideas, and the trust which all the players except Carrington reposed in him.

The Commonwealth Observer Group in Rhodesia's independence elections, charged with the responsibility of ascertaining impartially whether the elections were free and fair, was by far the largest and most ambitious Commonwealth operation ever attempted in the field. It also proved to be a landmark in election observation, setting a new benchmark in comprehensiveness and in proactively ensuring a level playing field for all the parties. The British opposed the very idea of a Commonwealth Group, worried that it might complicate their own supervision of the elections and restrict their freedom of manoeuvre. They wanted separate national teams from selected Commonwealth countries, each comprising only a few individuals. A fierce argument arose. Sonny argued strongly that the Lusaka Accord itself envisaged a collective role for a Commonwealth Group; indeed, the fraught situation within Rhodesia demanded no less. With overwhelming support from the rest of the Commonwealth, he was able to carry the day.

In his briefing to the group before it left for Salisbury, Sonny emphasised that although it would have no executive role, the Commonwealth would expect it to use its good offices in the cause of free and fair elections. The Observer Group did so with great effect, giving counsel on many matters to the Governor Lord Soames (who at one stage seemed inclined to ban Mugabe's ZANU (PF) from contesting the election), maintaining close contact with Sir John Boynton, the British Election Commissioner, listening to complaints from political parties and generally instilling confidence among a wide section of the populace by travelling widely in the country and observing for itself the situation on the ground. The whole exercise was of course fraught with risk, including the possibility of malpractice and even repudiation of the outcome by the Rhodesian security forces. By its presence, scale and style of operation, the Group exercised a reassuring and stabilising influence, building confidence in the country that the electoral process would be fair and the poll secret. I still remember our astonishment when Mugabe, on the very eve of the poll, revealed his ignorance of election procedures. He complained that there were going to be nine ballot boxes at the polling stations, one for each party: how each individual was voting would therefore get known. We assured him that there would be only one ballot box, ensuring secrecy of the ballot.

The group had to rely heavily on Ramphal's intervention to fullfil its mandate in the spirit intended at Lusaka. Having been forced to accept a Commonwealth Group, the British then tried to delay its arrival to prevent it from covering too much ground or acquiring too high a profile. The Governor also wanted to deny the group the additional staff it wished to have on the ground in order to cover actual polling in a comprehensive manner. On this, he was unyielding. The Chairman of the Observer Group thereupon told him that the group "would not be in a position to arrive at definitive conclusions on the conduct of the elections" if substantial additional staff were not allowed. The Governor still did not budge. The British Foreign Office only relented after Sonny elaborated on the damaging consequences if the group said its work had been impeded, and it was unable to give a clear verdict. 'The Mouse' again carried the day.

If Rhodesia demonstrated Sonny's skills in creative political footwork, South Africa stretched him even further. The apartheid regime was more firmly entrenched, the commercial interests of the UK and other developed countries much bigger. Punitive measures such as sanctions would hurt these interests and stimulate strong resistance. Most of the UK media were not on the Commonwealth's side, yet Sonny never lost heart or abandoned faith despite vitriolic criticism.

I have often wondered what drove Sonny Ramphal to champion the values and causes which were to dominate his tenure of office.

21

Racism is, of course, the negation of the Commonwealth's most fundamental value, just as racial equality is its very essence. Any equivocation on this principle would destroy the Commonwealth and Ramphal, like Arnold Smith, was always in the forefront to uphold it. However, it was not just an intellectual belief, but a deeply felt emotional one. It had something to do with his own background, the memory of his widowed great-grandmother's migration to Guyana as an indentured labourer to escape the discrimination and harshness with which Indian rural society treated widows, and the consciousness of what this new form of slavery must have entailed for her. There was, therefore, a very special passion whenever Sonny Ramphal spoke about issues of race, of apartheid, of subjugation and of exploitation. On this core value, Ramphal was not only immoveable but, when necessary, belligerent. Yet, while holding firm on principle, Ramphal was anxious to avoid splitting the Commonwealth. There were many who felt that Mrs Thatcher's attitudes on South Africa were tinged with racism, reinforced by Denis Thatcher's own predilections. But in taking on Mrs Thatcher, Ramphal did careful political homework in advance, in order to forge a seamless partnership between all the remaining Commonwealth countries, developed and developing. Ramphal's voice by itself would have been of little avail, but with the backing of all its members bar one, it could not be brushed aside. In a television interview given some months before he died, Denis Thatcher complained of that damned nuisance of a man called Ramphal, who was forever agitating the anti-apartheid cause. When asked for his reaction, Sonny said it was a compliment, proof that his own efforts had been effective.

The turning point was the idea of sending a Commonwealth Eminent Persons' Group to South Africa to mediate and kickstart a negotiated settlement between the apartheid regime and representatives of the black majority. It was floated by Prime Minister Hawke to Sonny during his pre-CHOGM visit to Australia. It bristled with difficulties and Sonny was quick to draw Bob Hawke's attention to them. Would such a group be viewed by African Commonwealth leaders and, more importantly, by blacks within South Africa as one more delaying tactic to blunt the international campaign against apartheid? Could the apartheid regime be trusted? How would the African National Congress and the United Democratic Front view it, and would they cooperate with the group? Would the apartheid regime itself countenance an external interference in its affairs? After anxious discussion, it was left to Mr. Hawke to float the idea at Nassau and for Sonny to prepare the ground. If Britain agreed to take part in the mission, it would be much more difficult for the South African Government to reject it. More problematic was the issue of securing African endorsement and cooperation. Sonny was ever mindful of the paramount need to keep Britain in play and to avoid any split between Britain and the rest. Despite strenuous African misgivings, he was able to bring them round to the view that a full-blown regime of sanctions could be postponed in order to keep Britain on board, at the same time trying to open the way for a negotiated settlement by talking to the apartheid regime. If the Eminent Persons Group failed, Britain would find it much harder to resist the call for punitive measures.

I was asked to lead the Secretariat team and entrusted with the task, along with my colleague Hugh Craft, to go and talk to the black South African leadership. Both of us went with a feeling of trepidation. Through friendly interlocutors, we were able to meet many of the prominent black figures, including Winnie Mandela, Trevor Manuel, Desmond Tutu, Allan Boesak and Azhar Cachalia among others. We encountered considerable cynicism about the initiative. All urged a tightening of sanctions. They rejected the argument that sanctions would hurt the blacks most. "We are hurting so much already that we will gladly accept more hurt if our pain can be brought to an end sooner" was the common refrain. We explained why they should cooperate with the group. If it succeeded, it would open the door to negotiations and the release of political prisoners. If it failed, the international campaign for sanctions would receive a boost. Given the tight six month time frame which was envisaged, this could not be a tactic of delay. I was delighted to report back to Sonny that black opposition had given way to sceptical cooperation.

Although the group's mission failed, it elaborated the formula and set in motion the chain of events that led to the release of Nelson Mandela and his colleagues and the negotiated settlement which followed. In recognition of the freedom movement's debt to the Commonwealth and to Sonny Ramphal personally, Nelson Mandela's first engagement in London following his release was an emotional reception hosted by Sonny in his Mayfair home. Winnie had become my friend after our repeated meetings in South Africa. Nelson I had met only once in Pollsmoor prison. As Winnie and I hugged each other, Nelson tapped me gently on the shoulder. "Do you remember me?" he asked.

The political issues which dominated his tenure of office are relatively well-known. Less well-known are Ramphal's efforts to extend the scope of Commonwealth functional cooperation as well as the capacity of the Secretariat to meet the needs of its developing member countries. Sonny was clear that the Commonwealth would have to pursue two parallel but linked agendas: on the one hand, the high politics of Southern Africa and the struggle against racism; on the other, a solid and growing contribution to the development efforts of its members.

On the development front some battles were won, others lost. The issue of Commonwealth student mobility became a flashpoint after Mrs Thatcher's decision to introduce full cost fees for all non-EU overseas students. This threatened to cut a vital link in Commonwealth relationships, fostered by the age old tradition of students coming to the UK for their higher studies. The three golden threads of the Commonwealth connection, Sonny argued, were the English language, the common law and Commonwealth student mobility. The imposition of full cost fees on Commonwealth students would cause lasting damage. His appeals fell on deaf ears. Despite strenuous efforts at successive Commonwealth Education Ministers' meetings, aided by the work of the Commonwealth Standing Committee on Student Mobility, Britain did not budge. I remember suggesting informally to Peter Brooke, the then Secretary of State for Education, that Britain should consider earmarking a portion of its overseas aid budget to cover the additional costs which full cost fees would entail for Commonwealth students, thereby assuaging Commonwealth anger as well as preserving Britain's position as the destination of choice for Commonwealth students. This too did not find favour. The consequence was a sharp decline in student flows to the UK, especially from the poorer developing ones. In the case of India, for example, a decisive and accelerating shift began to the United States, a phenomenon which the UK has been trying to counter in recent years through an enlarged scholarships programme. Although Indian student flows to the UK have increased, the tide continues to run strongly in the direction of the United States, and more recently to Australia.

There was only one positive outcome from this unhappy development. The idea of establishing a full-fledged independent degree-awarding Commonwealth Open University was canvassed. It appealed to Sonny, who put his weight behind it. Alas, it was felt to be too ambitious an idea. As a compromise, the Commonwealth of Learning was established, with its headquarters in Vancouver, to promote Commonwealth cooperation in distance learning. This new multilateral institution is perhaps the most lasting legacy of the Ramphal years to Commonwealth functional cooperation.

The Commonwealth Fund for Technical Cooperation, established during Arnold Smith's tenure, also grew, but not substantially. It nevertheless gave some modest additional credibility to the Commonwealth as a development organisation. Within the Secretariat itself, Sonny successfully pushed for new programmes to be instituted in the fields of industrial development, food production and management development, together with a more high profile women's development programme backed by regular meetings of Commonwealth Ministers for Women's Affairs.

Towards the end of Ramphal's tenure, it was apparent that the major financial contributors wished the Secretariat to be cut to size to give priority to other issues, such as human rights, democracy promotion, and better governance. Sonny's departure made it easier for them to weaken the Secretariat's developmental role, ignoring the link between the promotion of democracy and development. They were uncomfortable with the profile it had acquired under his leadership and the demand for more resources to aid its development efforts.

Although he was intensely serious in relation to his work, no account of life in Marlborough House with Sonny would be complete without some reference to the other side of his personality. He radiated an infectious joie de vivre, a sense of fun, a love of food and the other good things of life. His appetite for shopping was insatiable. India was his favourite shopping haunt and he would take out as much time as he could during visits to Delhi to trawl the shops and unearth hidden treasures. Jackie Kennedy is said never to have bought anything as a single item even when buying for herself. Sonny was a bit like her in this respect. Almost everything would be purchased in multiple numbers – not, as in Jackie's case, for himself alone, but for his extended family and friends. His annual Christmas party for the staff was always a hoot, with Sonny on the dance floor till the very end. Smaller parties at his house were filled with bonhomie and laughter. Even the annual Commonwealth Day Reception at Marlborough House, to which the Queen and Prince Philip came, had a quality of liveliness far removed from the normal diplomatic receptions to which London is accustomed, or the formality which the presence of royalty seems to demand. Often there would be a steel band. Always there would be a potent rum punch, served out of an enormous silver punch bowl specially manufactured in India for the occasion. His butler Indal would not consider his duty to be done if at least some of Sonny's guests did not find it difficult to leave without physical help.

Accompanying Sonny on his visits to Commonwealth countries was a wonderful mix of work and fun. On his first official visit to Sri Lanka, he expressed a wish to go duck shooting. We were ferried by helicopter to some spot a short distance from Colombo and, with army help, driven to the shooting venue. There was much excitement as successive waves of ducks rose in the air. Sonny ran all over the place, gun blazing, but the ducks all got away. We were consoled at a Sri Lankan army camp with the most delicious crab curry I have ever eaten.

In New Zealand, an opportunity arose to go trout fishing in a lake. Apart from Sonny and myself, there was my colleague Henry Lynch Shyllon from Sierra Leone. He had clearly never been fishing before because he came dressed in a three-piece suit. Arriving at the lake, he said that he did not know how to swim and would therefore not take the risk of going out to fish in a boat: he would prefer to stay on the shore, rod in hand. Sonny's enthusiasm had brought him this far, but could take him no farther.

In Barbados, during a meeting of Commonwealth Finance Ministers, some staff members wished to go for a midnight swim in the sea. Would Sonny come too? Of course he did, but stayed in shallow water. We discovered he was not a swimmer, but he was always a good sport.

Towards the end of his tenure of office, I accompanied Sonny on my first visit to Guyana. He showed me around Georgetown with mixed feelings: pride at its splendid wooden architecture, regret at the run-down condition of the city, embarrassment at the yellow coloured tap water and the extreme shortage of toilet paper.

It was Diwali. It was a joy to see it celebrated as it must have been in India a century ago. Everywhere, Indian homes were lit only with little 'diyas', the traditional earthen oil wick lamps, without any of the garish electric lighting that you now often see in India. Nor were there any firecracker explosions which have made Diwali a festival of noise as much as of light in its home country. In Georgetown there was only illumination, and silence.

Sonny insisted that we go into the interior to do some fishing. The river teemed with piranha and I wondered how quickly they would devour me if I fell into the water. It turned out to be the easiest fishing of my life. Piranha after piranha was landed, with each piranha adding to the smile on Sonny's face. If only it could have been as easy to land some of the political piranhas he had to deal with!

Most memorable of all was a visit to Delhi during the festival of Holi, which is celebrated in North India with riotous abandon. Everyone is free to throw colour at everyone else or spray them with coloured water. We arrived at the Holi celebration hosted by the proprietors of the Times of India. Huge vats lined the garden, each filled with water of a different colour. Some of the guests were being hoisted and dunked right into the vats, emerging out of them looking like bedraggled nothings-on-earth. Sonny looked worried. He was relieved when a young woman came up to him and proceeded to smear his face with what he thought was colour but was in fact oily, sticky, jet-black paint. When she finished, Sonny looked as if he was about to step on to the stage to play the darkest-ever Othello. Many more layers of vivid reds, blues and purples soon adorned all of us. Returning to our hotel, Sonny got the shock of his life when he saw himself in the lift's mirror. The rest of us could not stop laughing. "But I have to see Rajiv (Gandhi) later this afternoon", he said plaintively. "How on earth will I get all this off?" His scrub down was only partially successful. Rajiv, too, had a good laugh when he saw him.

At a personal level, Sonny's biggest disappointment was the failure of his candidacy in 1981 for the post of UN Secretary-General. Brian

Urquhart had warned him that this was not a competitive exam, designed to choose the best man. He took his defeat gracefully, and returned from New York to plunge with renewed vigour into his Commonwealth endeavours. The UN's loss was the Commonwealth's gain.

At the end of his 15 years as Secretary-General, rich tributes were paid to Sonny by the Commonwealth's political leaders. Sir Lynden Pindling, Prime Minister of the Bahamas, said Sonny had swept the Commonwealth off its feet, as a young suitor would a damsel. He had taken her to the dance floor, and taught her how to dance. They were made for each other.

The Commonwealth waits expectantly for another suitor like Sonny Ramphal.

Shridath "Sonny" Ramphal: part-Asian, part-African, part-European, part-Native American but totally Caribbean

Rex Nettleford

— ∞ —

The typical West Indian, goes the saying, is "part-African, part-European, part-Asian, part-Native American but totally Caribbean." To those accustomed to manipulate power from homogeneous bases and to exercise hegemony over others deemed to be children of a lesser god, such a chaotic mix of disparate elements is difficult to comprehend, let alone figure out, for acceptance.

Shridath "Sonny" Ramphal is typically West Indian. He couldn't be otherwise coming as he does from Guyana with its Rupununi hinterland of Amerindians, its large population of the offspring of Indian indentured servants brought in after Emancipation to replace the once enslaved Africans whose descendants still tenant Guyana, and its strong European (British) influences rooted in colonial conditioning through grammar school and university education – the latter pursued in Shridath Ramphal's time in the United Kingdom itself.

The texture of character and the sophistication of sense and sensibility engaging the Planet's systemic contradictions were ironically colonialism's benefits for a couple of generations in the West Indies. In dealing with the dilemma of difference manifested in the ability to assert without rancour, to draw on a sense of rightness

— ∞ —

Professor Rex Nettleford, emeritus Vice-Chancellor of the University of the West Indies, is a major cultural figure in the contemporary Caribbean, known for his many books and as founder of the National Dance Theatre Company of Jamaica.

without hubris, to remain human(e) in the face of persistent obscenities that plague the human condition, all such attributes in turn served to endow the Caribbean man with the conviction that Planet Earth is, in the end, one world to share. The interdependence of the Earth's tenants dictate a quest for cooperation and unity in diversity – a psychic balance at the crossroads as it were.

What better qualification could anyone have expected for the iconic role Sir Shridath Ramphal was to play in the quest since the mid-20th century for peace, tolerance, equity, mutual respect and understanding between peoples as well as trust and an undying faith in the human being's capacity for survival against all odds?

Honed in the microcosm that is his native West Indies, Shridath Ramphal acquired not only the experience and skill at negotiating place and purpose in the creative chaos that was daily existence in the progress from the self government struggle to Independence. He also shared a moral authority in determining directions to zones of comfort and positive action by stakeholders intent on becoming the creators of their own destiny.

His many years as a trusted international public servant – as Secretary-General of the Commonwealth of nations, as well as the wide experience gained as Co-Chair of the International Commission on Global Governance, and as member of similar Commissions that followed, as Chairman of the West Indian Commission, as a governor of the prestigious International Development Research Centre that seminal development assistance agency located in Ottawa, Canada, as Special Adviser to the Earth Summit and more recently as moving spirit and chief negotiator of the CARICOM Regional Negotiating Machinery in response to the far-reaching challenges of globalisation, as well as one of the negotiators who brought to a successful conclusion discussions on the Belize-Guatemala border dispute (to name only some of the areas in which his enormous talents have been utilised) – have all contributed to his towering wisdom, his iconic intellectual stature and his unique vision of the future of Planet Earth which, in his own words, is but "one world to share,"[1] and not a piece of real estate to be parcelled out by conquest and claims to "prior discovery" and "effective occupation" backed up by Papal Bulls.

It is his vision of a **Caribbean** world, engaging the wider Planet without loss of a sense of the inner logic and consistency of his West Indian world, which has marked him off as the 21st century citizen that the Third Millennium requires leaders and all progressive tenants of the Planet to be. His chairmanship of the West Indian Commission was vintage Ramphal. He brought to it all the sophistication, sustained and tireless application, textured sense and sensibility that his region requires of all his compatriots harnessed into public service.

In presenting the commission's report[2] which he cleverly crafted he tried to get CARICOM leaders to see their region "beyond themselves" without harbouring schizophrenic fears of irreconcilable contradictions and pluralistic confusion. The West Indian Commission, he assured them:

> *"is not hesitant in asserting that beginning the process of integration of the entire Caribbean Basin is the most important Caribbean idea, and could be the most important Caribbean enterprise, since Columbus condemned us to a history of European domination and a density bound up with European nationalism. We see nothing whatever incompatible with the pursuit of that idea and enterprise and the importance, indeed the need, for us to sustain and strengthen our intimate relationships as immediate family. From our corner of the Caribbean we must reach out to the wider community in and around the Caribbean archipelago across the barriers of sea and language, of cultures and systems, rejecting the separatisms imposed on the region by the conquests that began five hundred years ago, responding to the reality for which Jose Marti found eloquent words a century ago when he asserted 'we must save ourselves together, or together we will disappear'."[3]*

Whether the Caricom leaders all fell for this remarkable mix of scholarship, the appeal to history, and seductive oratory was very much in doubt. Some leaders clearly understood. Others may well have found it difficult to fathom the density and interconnectivity of the issues impacting on regional integration and the relationship with the newly globalised world which Shridath Ramphal certainly understood, having presided over a Commonwealth that is multi-layered, multi-faceted, multi-cultural and multi-racial and covering countries and regions plagued by all the big issues of development from poverty through healthcare deficiencies to educational deficit.

Still others seemed daunted by the challenge, as outlined by the guru of a teacher that Shridath Ramphal, in his disquisitions, could appear to be. A particular politician took objection to being treated as a student: the lecturer was too prescient, too demanding, for comfort. In effect, the recommendations were not really accepted and here some of the finest qualities of this practical Caribbean man of experience shone through. Like some of the other members of the commission he guessed that in time, his compatriots would see the light. Many of the rejected recommendations were to later creep into CARICOM strategies.

Ramphal patiently waited, responded with grace under the pressure of rejection, but stuck to what he knew history and existential reality were saying.

"Five hundred years after Columbus we have a primordial mandate to demonstrate our own capacity to change our fortunes and our destiny".[4]

He was after all walking the path marked out by the likes of Marcus Mosiah Garvey, Norman Washington Manley, Eric Williams, Jose Marti and all such founding fathers of the Caribbean. Such was the pedigree of his faith in the sure salvation of his Caribbean which he was helping to build and shape. He turned to St. Lucian Nobel Laureate Derek Walcott citing the poet's masterwork **Omeros** – "why waste lines on Achille a shade on the seafloor? Because as self healing coral a quiet culture is branching from the white ribs of each ancestor deeper than it seems on the surface; slowly but sure, it will change us with the fluent sculpture of Time."[5] Consistent with the changes history has wrought upon us, "Mr. Chairman, President, Prime Ministers, the West Indian Commission invites you to agree and to decide to act[6]," he pleaded, for this was a **time for action**.

No one could ever accuse Shridath Ramphal of not being a man of action. The quality of service which attended all such action has been of particular importance to the Caribbean region, especially in his work with the University of the West Indies, a primary agent of regional integration and post colonial certitude which he served as Chancellor for all of fourteen years.[7] It is significant that he served simultaneously as Chancellor of the University of Guyana and Warwick University (UK). Tens of thousands at UWI will remember him for the indefatigable patience and grace with which he would personally congratulate and shake the hand of each graduand at every graduation ceremony over the period – a marathon performance worthy of any Book of Records.

Man of action that he always was, Shridath Ramphal was not slow to grasp the implications of the UWI's own initiative (the UWI Distance Education, UWIDITE facility) in responding to the growing challenge to developing countries to provide greater access to higher education for their populations. With the support of fellow West Indians Sir Roy Marshall, Dr James Maraj and Barbadian Prime Minister Erskine Sandiford, Commonwealth Secretary- General Ramphal threw the Secretariat's support behind what was to become the Commonwealth of Learning (COL) headquartered in Vancouver, Canada. This followed on recommendations by an initial Committee set up by Shridath Ramphal under the chairmanship of Lord Asa Briggs with a subsequent Working Group to develop the eventual structures. Two UWI academics were to be members of both the initial Committee and The Working Group.[8]

In a UWI 40th Anniversary address in 1988 Chancellor Ramphal was able to remind his listeners that "Universities everywhere are coming to terms with the reality that they have lost their traditional monopoly of knowledge accumulation, generation and dissemination. The future will in part consist of working in partnership with others engaged in the knowledge, information and learning industry".[9] This is, today, part of the thrust of the University of the West Indies Administration's strategic planning.

His vision 20 years ago was that:

> *"One day the Commonwealth Of Learning, working with and through UWIDITE, can ensure that any learner anywhere in the West Indies should be able to study any distance teaching programme available from any bona fide college or university in the entire Commonwealth: to ensure, in short, by harnessing communication technology, that tertiary (and even vocational) education of the highest quality available in the Commonwealth through distance learning techniques is brought within reach of every West Indian whatever his or her age, or resources, or occupation, whether in Belmopan or Basseterre, in New Providence or Point Saline or Port Morant, in Scarborough or Spanish Town. In this*

enterprise, the University of the West Indies will be, of course, a receiver, but you will be a giver also to the Pacific, to Africa, even to the open learning institutions of the developed Commonwealth. Three generations and more ago, West Indians of ambition reached out to learning through lamplight and correspondence courses. Tomorrow they must be able to reach even farther, through satellite and radio and television, through programmes centred here in the University of the West Indies backed up by the Commonwealth of Learning."[10]

The University of the West Indies, has been the lucky beneficiary of the Ramphal grasp of global governance, of the man's deep understanding of a world that is changing as if in contest with the speed of light, and of his recognition of the need for skills which a developing country institution like the UWI must produce, so that its graduates can find firm place and sustained purpose in the 'knowledge society' of the third millennium, even while maintaining standards and delivering education of excellence. This came through strongly in the commission he set up to look into the renewal and transformation of the University of the West Indies – a move which has guided the institution over the past decade in its strategic thrust into the future. The commission pointed the university toward a programme of action for the way forward intellectually and structurally, with provision for flexibility, adaptability and on-going change.

During the 2003-2004 academic year the UWI was fortunate to have had him visit all 15 countries served by the university, under a programme known as 'The Chancellor's Forum.' He held meetings with senior public servants, academics, private sector leaders, civil society activists and the media, sharing views with them on the various and complex aspects of global governance. The response to what was soon realised to be a special added gift to the university was overwhelming.

The UWI continues to take seriously Shridath Ramphal's observation that:
*"The university, in one sense, is a purveyor of enlightenment; but in another, more primary sense it is by its very being a symbol of society's enlightenment, in this case, a symbol of our enlightened acknowledgement of a **uniting West Indian identity** – that oneness that is so dear to West Indians in Brixton or Brooklyn but so easily blurred at home."*

And as if to give cogency to the pedigree of the region's premier institution of higher learning, Chancellor Ramphal further stated that:

"the university has helped to give back to the region a sense of pride and self-knowledge, forming and strengthening that belief in ourselves which the political process of decolonisation made fully possible".[11]

Chancellor Ramphal also understood the need for universities to place great emphasis on the exercise of the creative attributes of the mind. The challenges of politics, economics, social development in the new global situation he felt demanded no less. In his 1988 Warwick University Lectures on Development he reminded his listeners that the "rigidity of disciplines is unhelpful: what the scientist sees as valuable technological advance may be seen by the economist as economically unviable; and what the economist sees as viable may be seen as plainly nonsensical by the ecologist." Indeed, the clearing of "non-productive" mangroves to build hotels that would provide jobs and attract foreign exchange for a revenue-strapped economy may bring ecological disaster following a hurricane or tsunami. In those lectures the Chancellor warned that we would have nothing to be proud of "if our science, at the pinnacle of its achievement, threatens not to save but to sacrifice us." Both Warwick University and the University of the West Indies might well have benefited from the warning.[12]

As Vice Chancellor I had cause to say some years ago:

"The University of the West Indies is deeply indebted to Sir Shridath for his guidance, for the generous sharing of his years of experience in engaging the big issues of the wider world, and for his unfailing commitment to the cause of education as the path to individual empowerment, to national and regional sovereignty and to the promise of a better world. The UWI is proud to have had him as our Chancellor and wishes for him many more productive years in which he can continue to contribute to our region – the microcosm of that 'brave new world' that his optimism and demonstrated capacity for action over the elegance and eloquence of rhetoric, have helped to make us all believe awaits us.

We are, indeed, deeply in the debt of this dedicated, faithful public servant, this wise and generous mentor to many, this industrious, tireless man-of-action, this brilliant advocate and negotiator,

Distinguished Fellow in the School of Graduate Studies and Chancellor Emeritus".[13]

His capacity for action, but more importantly, his grasp of the character of the kind of realigned world in formation, with serious threats of retaining old obscenities, forced the leaders of the Caribbean Community to engage his services as head of the Regional Negotiating Machinery. That, too, brought to the Caribbean Presence in the European and North American fora a certain coherence and sense of unity now accepted as part of Caricom's **modus operandi** in the globalised world. It is a contribution that cannot be taken lightly and it remains a legacy in the repositioning of former colonial outposts in the new configuration of the global playing field which, while still not "level," provides some flexibility of movement in negotiating the space available to a region like the Caribbean.

Shridath Ramphal would be the first to admit that not all his efforts have been successful at having the world, including his Caribbean, see the world his way. But disappointments have by no means made him into a victim of cynicism, pessimism or despair. Small wonder this was duly recognized by those who recommended him for the 2002 Indira Gandhi Prize for Peace, Disarmament and Development in acknowledgement of a lifelong active career dedicated to the cause of international understanding and development.[14] He had after all lived and laboured for enlarging freedom for humankind, freedom from want and fear, and from various forms of prejudice and narrowness. His contribution to the struggle against apartheid while serving as Commonwealth Secretary-General immediately comes to mind.

As the big issues reared their debilitating heads, eyes turned to the man from the Caribbean – Shridath Ramphal – for advice and guidance. He cannot be forgotten in the recent recognition by the Nobel Prize selectors of those who have contributed positively to the dialogue on climate change. The international programme to promote Leadership for Environment and Development (LEAD) is no doubt connected to the invitation extended to him to serve as Special Advisor to the Secretary-General of the Earth Summit in 1992 and he cast a long shadow ever after, leading up to the time of the Asian tsunami and the accompanying massive destruction of life, property and the environment years later.

It is an interesting paradox that journalistic reports have come out praising former US Vice President Al Gore, part winner of the 2007 Nobel Prize for his fight against global warming and climate change, as he spoke to a Caribbean conference in the Turks and Caicos Islands. He stressed that the region faces the threat of economic disaster from climate change, what with the increasing dependency by Caribbean people on tourism, sun, sea and golden beaches. The report went on to observe that "Scientists have warned that the Caribbean, where more than half the population live within a mile of the coast, faces particular risks from climate change, including stronger hurricanes, more frequent droughts and damage to vital reefs and mangroves."[15] The news report did not inform its readers that the organisation (the IPCC) that shared equally the Nobel Prize with Gore had as part of its research team three academics from the University of the West Indies (one from each of the three campuses) – the same university over which Shridath Ramphal presided as Chancellor for a decade and more.

More importantly, Shridath Ramphal had long brought to the attention of the hundreds who heard him the dangers of environmental degradation to development. If some people wondered what all the talk about environmental integrity has to do with small island and developing country states, especially since the poor in those states are not the ones polluting rivers with effluent from factories which they do not own and are not the ones using fossil fuels that induce global warming, Shridath Ramphal had no reason to wonder. He was able to tell the IDB back in 2000 that "global warming exposes the Caribbean to more frequent and more intensive storm surges and to sea-level rise."[16] Such natural disasters are indeed the bane of Caribbean governments which face the Sisyphean spectre of two steps forward and three back with the periodical destruction of physical infrastructure and loss of income by the mass of their populations. According to Shridath Ramphal "In the last five years [between 1996 and 2000] 44 hurricanes have roared through or past the region".

He said something that is of further significance to the West Indian Diaspora among others. His native Guyana, which is below sea level, is endangered: "the Dutch and the British who colonised Guyana used thousands of African slaves and Indian indentured labourers to protect low-lying land from the sea before planting the sugar that made Guyana an imperial asset. It would be a cruel twist of fate if the dilapidated sea wall of Guyana's polders were now to overflow because in Holland and Britain, and elsewhere in the industrialised world, the affluence to which sugar contributed, introduced patterns of fossil fuel consumption that eventually cause the seas to rise in the distant Caribbean."[17]

Shridath Ramphal, the internationalist Caribbean man, knows that this is no basis for the self-respect and self-esteem after which the sons and daughters of the underdeveloped segment of humanity, hanker. They wish to be recognised stakeholders and owners of the process of sustainability required of both the policies and the vision informing such policies that will give them protection against natural disasters as much as against the obscenities of corrupt political rulers and shortsighted developmentalists.

To achieve this Shridath Ramphal knows from experience in, and of, the real world that none of this is possible without the admittance of human agency into a world facing the threat of extinction and self-destruction. But as he warns, "time is short. [T]he world faces a kind of unspoken ultimatum; either we go forward to a more ordered world governed by the value of caring and tolerance, a world of mutual rights and responsibilities, one of rules and laws which all respect, a more democratic world with power constrained in the interest of all or, ironically, freed of the constraints of the Cold War, we may regress to a world without values save those of self, and without vision save that of paramountcy, a world ruled by power not by law, [but] one in which the few who prosper matter more than the many who are poor....the global reality is that co-operation has become not merely a virtuous option but a necessary condition of survival. A world which rejects cooperation will become one of spiralling chaos and ultimate self-destruction."[18]

Such a mission/vision for human growth and development is recommended not only to Western Christians engaging Middle Eastern Muslims, nor to Black Africans and their descendants engaging a racist white North Atlantic, not only to Asians and their indentured offspring engaging the descendants of those who greedily exploited vulnerable labour forces from Mother India, China and Africa, not only to indigenous Native Americans still struggling for their lands later usurped by conquering intruders, and not only to a 53 nation Commonwealth on which the sun never sets as it houses a variety of ethnic/language groups and persons of diverse religious persuasions.

His recommendation is no less addressed to his native Caribbean which remains the living laboratory of exploration and experimentation, in both human relations and cultural diversity, following on the encounters over half a millennium between Europe, Africa, Asia and the Levantine and all of these in turn with the indigenous peoples who had settled the Americas time out of mind, and had discovered Columbus on that Bahamian island in 1492. For this is the space in which Shridath "Sonny" Ramphal was reared into the textured, sophisticated, sagacious and clever human being he was to become -- being part-Asian, part-European, part-African, part-Native American, but totally Caribbean.

Heterogeneity, not homogeneity, is here the guiding principle of social organisation not only for Shridath Ramphal's Caribbean but also for all of Planet Earth!

1   S. Ramphal, *One World to Share: Selected Speeches of the Commonwealth Secretary-General 1975-1978*. Century Benham, 1979

2   *Time For Action: Report of the West Indian Commission*. Black Rock, Barbados, West Indian Commission 1992. See also Hilbourne Watson: "Caribbean Integration under Global neo-Liberalism: Selected Issues in the West Indian Commission Report in 21st Century Policy Review – An American Caribbean and African Forum, Spring 1994, IDO Publications.

3   S. Ramphal, "Time to Act". *Caribbean Quarterly Monograph: Sir Shridath Ramphal – Contributions to Caribbean Quarterly*, p.67 (reproduced from CQ Vol. 39, no. 1, 1993)

4   Ibid p.72

5   Ibid

6   Ibid

7   Shridath Ramphal was Chancellor of the University of the West Indies for fourteen years – from 1990 to 2004. Before him were Sir Hugh Wooding and Sir Allen Lewis as native Chancellors following on the long tenure of the first Chancellor Princess Alice, Countess of Athlone.

8   The two UWI academics involved were Professor Rex Nettleford who sat on the Briggs Committee and Pro Vice Chancellor, Professor Gerald Lalor, founder of UWIDITE who was a member of the Working Group.

9   S. Ramphal "Vivat, Floreat, Crescat" – UWI 40th Anniversary Convocation Address in *Caribbean Quarterly Monograph*, p.53 (reproduced from Caribbean Quarterly Vol. 35 No. 3, 1989)

10 Ibid

11 Ibid

12 S. Ramphal, *The Warwick University Lectures on Development 1988*. Cited in Rex Nettleford's – *Inward Stretch, Outward Reach: A Voice from the Caribbean*. Macmillan 1993, p. 177

13 Rex Nettleford, Preface to *Caribbean Quarterly Monograph*, p.iv

14 The Indira Gandhi Prize for Peace, Disarmament and Development is administered by the Indira Gandhi Memorial Trust to commemorate Indira Gandhi's outstanding contribution to national and global well-being. Previous awardees included Vaclav Havel, Trevor Huddleston, Mikael Gorbachev, Gro Harlem Brundtland, Muhammand Yunus and Mary Robinson. The Prize was presented to Sir Shridath in New Delhi in November of 2003.

15 See "Gore calls on Caribbean Islands to unite on global warming threat" in *The Barbados Advocate*, Thursday, November 22, 2007 p.15

16 S. Ramphal, *Is 2000 a Time for Caribbean Reflection*, Cátedra Siglo XXI Lecture Series, Inter-American Development Bank, Washington, D.C., 2 August 2000

17 Ibid

18 S. Ramphal, "World Language Opportunities, Challenges, Responsibilities". *Caribbean Quarterly Monograph*, pp77/78   (reproduced from CQ Vol. 42, No. 4, 1993)

Ramphal and Southern Africa

— ∞ —

Ramphal and the independence of Zimbabwe

Patsy Robertson

When Shridath (Sonny) Ramphal walked into the courtyard of the Commonwealth Secretariat's Headquarters at Marlborough House in London in the summer of 1975 as the second Secretary-General of the Commonwealth, he was already a seasoned practitioner in the international effort to mobilise world opinion against the entrenchment of racism in southern Africa.

He had the advantages that a multiracial, multicultural West Indian background invested in its people. These included an excellent basic education, enhanced, in his case, by law studies at King's College, London and membership of Grays Inn. Like others of his West Indian generation, he was born in colonial times but grew up with the knowledge that capable West Indians, such as his father J I Ramphal who was the first local Labour Commissioner in Guyana, were managing some of their country's affairs with distinction. This early experience gave him the confidence that West Indians were capable of governing themselves and contributing to problem solving in the wider international community. The racial mix of the West Indies, especially his native Guyana, where children of all races rubbed shoulders in the classroom, played games together in the school grounds, attended the same parties, saw the same films and read the same books, established in his mind the equality of all races and respect for differences in religion.

— ∞ —

Patsy Robertson, formerly a Jamaican diplomat, joined the Commonwealth Secretariat soon after it was started and became spokesperson for Sonny Ramphal and Director of Information; she now chairs the Commonwealth Association of former employees of the Secretariat.

The people of the West Indies were keenly aware of the development of apartheid in South Africa. Pre-independent Jamaica, where he had practised law after the collapse of the Federation, was one of the first countries in the world to take action to ban entry to South African passport holders and, shortly after its attainment of independence in 1966, Guyana moved to the forefront of Caribbean countries in support of the banned African National Congress (ANC).

Ramphal had an early personal and bitter encounter with Rhodesian politics. In the celebrated and anti-colonialist law chambers of Dingle Foot in London, he had been an associate of Herbert Chitepo, already a rising political star in Rhodesia. Chitepo was later assassinated in the struggle against Ian Smith's illegal regime. Ramphal never forgot the fate of his friend, or what it meant for a future Zimbabwe.

As Guyana's Foreign Minister he had attended many Commonwealth meetings, held in the decade since 1965 when the Secretariat was established – the same year that Ian Smith made his infamous Unilateral Declaration of Independence (UDI) of Rhodesia. Commonwealth leaders knew him, and recognised that he played an important role in the ideas that Guyana advanced at their meetings. He had also established himself as an energetic supporter of attempts by newly emerging developing countries to make their mark on the international community. He facilitated his country's entry into the Non-Aligned Movement (NAM) and chaired the first meeting of NAM Foreign Ministers held in the western hemisphere in Guyana in 1972. He was also one of the architects of the formation of the African, Caribbean and Pacific (ACP) group to negotiate jointly trade and investment agreements with the then European Economic Community. And, he was a frequent player at the United Nations where he was twice Vice President of the Security Council.

He therefore brought to the service of the Commonwealth an unrivalled network of international contacts which would enable him to take the bold initiatives that characterised his 15 years at the helm of the world's uniquely internationalist grouping. He was also well aware that he was inheriting a mantle from the first Secretary-General, Arnold Smith of Canada, who had laid the foundation for the Commonwealth's principled opposition to Ian Smith's UDI; this was despite the attitude of the British Government, which regarded the white Southern Rhodesians as "kith and kin," and was resolved to take no action to overturn a patently illegal action designed to perpetuate white supremacy.

By the time that Ramphal walked through the doors of Marlborough House, six previous Heads of Government Meetings had been dominated by the Rhodesian question: Lagos (January 1966), London (September 1966) London (January 1969), Singapore (1971) Ottawa (1973) and Kingston (1975). In those years the Commonwealth had set up a Committee to press for sanctions against Rhodesia, and a training programme for refugees from Rhodesia. The UN Security Council had imposed comprehensive sanctions. The British Government had made several efforts to end the Rhodesia crisis. There were meetings on ships – *Tiger and Fearless* – between the British Prime Minister, Harold Wilson, and Ian Smith. The arrival of the Conservative Ted Heath in Downing Street, in June 1970, was followed by the announcement that his government was considering lifting the non-mandatory embargo on arms sales to South Africa. This created a huge row in the Commonwealth which led to a confrontation with Britain at the Singapore meeting the following January. That same year, Foreign Secretary Alec Douglas-Home signed the Anglo-Rhodesian settlement proposals with Ian Smith in Salisbury. This was based on the much derided 1969 constitution, and scarcely fitted in with the Six Principles agreed by Britain earlier. These principles enshrined the "principle and intention of unimpeded progress towards majority rule....."

The way for this agreement had been cleared by an earlier British envoy Lord Arnold Goodman, who had visited Salisbury several times to prepare the way for Home. When the accusation was made that the agreement sold out the Africans, he said: "The terms of settlement were not a sell-out. The African had been sold out long before"[1]. The following year in 1972, Lord Pierce was sent by the British Government to find out what Africans thought about the settlement and his report confirmed that a majority had rejected the settlement. In 1974, ZANU and ZAPU leaders Robert Mugabe and Joshua Nkomo were released from prison and the armed struggle intensified with Mugabe based in Mozambique and Nkomo in Zambia.

At the same time, there were intensive efforts being made by the Frontline States – Tanzania, Zambia, and Botswana, to broker some kind of internal settlement. In December 1974, the Lusaka Accord was signed and despite difficulties this led to talks between Smith and the leaders of the majority population of Rhodesia. One of the main negotiators was Bishop Abel Muzorewa. Britain was also active in setting up a special committee in Brussels to look into breaches of sanctions by EEC nationals.

A decade of frantic efforts to reach a settlement had borne little fruit. As he took up his post, Ramphal was mindful of the advice he had received from many leaders when he called on them as he was seeking to become Secretary General. Indira Gandhi in particular exhorted him to ensure that the Commonwealth realised its potential as an organisation which had articulated strongly its opposition to all forms of discrimination in the Singapore Declaration of Commonwealth Principles in 1971. With Ivan Head of Canada and Mark Chona of Zambia, Ramphal, as a member of Guyana's delegation, had played a central role at Singapore in drafting the declaration. In that document, besides condemning the wide disparities of wealth existing in the world, leaders pledged to use all their efforts to foster human equality and dignity everywhere and "recognised that racial discrimination is a dangerous sickness threatening the healthy development of the human race."

In 1975, Ramphal was ready for this task. One of his first acts was to warn leaders that conflicts could no longer be geographically contained; the possibility of a widening war in southern Africa would lead to a racial crisis worldwide. He reinforced this message in his first report to leaders in 1977. He wrote: "It was prudent as well as moral that all members of the Commonwealth should regard the struggle for justice in Southern Africa as their own struggle and exert themselves in their own interest towards a peaceful transfer of power in all of southern Africa into the hands of the majority of people there". He also knew that he had the full support of the great majority of Commonwealth leaders to press forward with Commonwealth action to support the liberation movements in southern Africa.

During his 15 years as Secretary-General, he developed close working relationships with such leaders as Malcolm Fraser and Bob Hawke of Australia, Pierre Trudeau and Brian Mulroney of Canada, Indira and Rajiv Gandhi of India, Julius Nyerere of Tanzania, Kenneth Kaunda of Zambia, Seretse Khama of Botswana, General Olusegun Obasanjo of

Nigeria, Michael Manley of Jamaica, Errol Barrow and Tom Adams of Barbados, Forbes Burnham of Guyana, Mohammad Mahathir of Malaysia, Lee Kuan Yew of Singapore and Ratu Kamasese Mara of Fiji. He was a trusted friend in the "political parlour" of each. And, these leaders were well-known internationally.

Ramphal was therefore able to position the Commonwealth Secretariat as a key adviser on economic, political and constitutional issues to the liberation movements in Southern Africa. He facilitated the attendance of Secretariat officials as observers at Commonwealth meetings and deployed the most experienced legal and economic experts employed by the Commonwealth Fund for Technical Cooperation. One of Ramphal's first tasks was to indicate to the newly independent government of Mozambique that (though not a member state) the Commonwealth planned to take immediate practical steps to assist the country in its intention to implement sanctions against Rhodesia.

In March 1976 Ramphal was invited to visit Mozambique to discuss the needs of the country after nearly two decades of a proxy war backed by South Africa. It was clear that the country was suffering from the effects of the sanctions against Rhodesia. There was a loss of revenue and foreign exchange, as well as export credits. Food including maize, beef, wheat and rice, was in short supply. The war had led to the dislocation of millions of people and there was a need for technical assistance to help with the consequences of the closure of the border with Rhodesia. From Mozambique, Ramphal then went to the United Nations to discuss the situation there with UN Secretary General Kurt Waldheim, who had continued to recognise the Commonwealth's role in supporting the UN's global efforts on peace and security issues as well as providing practical assistance to a significant number of UN member states.

Ramphal reported on his visit to Mozambique to the Commonwealth's Sanctions Committee and the Commonwealth Heads of Government. The Sanctions Committee recommended that a special technical assistance programme for Mozambique should be established. While modest, the Special Fund of £1 million for a two to three year programme, was able to finance the training of teachers, doctors, lecturers at the university, nursing tutors and other medical and technical personnel. The CFTC was also able to undertake four export market studies to help in developing the export trade, and a pre-feasibility study on the improvement of the Mozambican port of Beira. A senior CFTC expert was also seconded to the UN Secretary-General's technical mission to Mozambique which estimated that the country would need hundreds of millions of dollars for each of the two years following the closure of the border with Rhodesia. Almost 10 years later, of course, Mozambique joined the Commonwealth – the first ex-Portuguese colony to do so.

The Secretariat had initiated in 1966 a programme of assistance to suitably qualified people who had left Rhodesia to obtain education and training. Working with member Governments, the Secretariat also coordinated the programme of assistance with the OAU, UN agencies, nationalist organizations and a number of voluntary bodies. Since 1966 more than 2,800 Zimbabweans had been offered study places, scholarships and employment as a result of offers made by 25 Commonweath governments. The Secretariat also administered the Commonwealth Rhodesia Scholarship Trust Fund, established in 1972 following a Canadian pledge to provide funds for those outside Rhodesia who had been accepted as students in institutions in Commonwealth developing countries. Under this fund, which also received contributions from Britain, Australia and New Zealand, some 229 students were able to study in 15 developing countries. The Special Programme provided correspondence education for Rhodesians at home with funds contributed by Australia and New Zealand, and 100 students signed up with a well established correspondence college in Britain which provided A level and first degree courses. By the time independence was gained, over 4,000 Zimbabweans had been helped to study places as a result of the contributions by some 25 Commonwealth countries.

By 1975, the situation in Rhodesia was noticeably deteriorating, with white emigration and a serious security situation. There was then a definite prospect of a more aggressive armed struggle. The collapse of the Portuguese dictatorship in April 1974, and the closure of the border with Mozambique meant that the intensification of sanctions had the possibility of damaging further the beleagured Rhodesian economy. South Africa, which had played a significant role in putting pressure on the Frontline States by sponsoring proxy wars in Mozambique and Angola, and by using its financial and military power to oppose any settlement that would give Africans a share in the governance of their country, had after a decade, decided to search for some kind of a rapprochement with its neighbouring African states. But South Africa was also facing demands for Namibia's independence, and the Commonwealth had also pledged to support Namibia in this struggle and had agreed that multi-lateral assistance should be made available to Namibians who had fled their country. Sam Nujoma, the Namibian leader, was no stranger to Ramphal. As Foreign Minister Ramphal had seen Guyana appointed the first Chairman of the UN's Council for Namibia.

All these pressures were felt by Ian Smith and made him agree to talks with leaders of the Rhodesia African National Congress at Victoria Falls in August 1975. President Kaunda and Prime Minister Vorster of South Africa were also present. The talks collapsed the following day due to Smith's refusal to grant immunity from arrest to the exiled ANC leaders. Smith then held a series of talks with Joshua Nkomo, from December 1975 to March 1976, but these also broke down because Smith refused to accept majority rule in a short period of time.

Meanwhile Britain continued to search for a solution and in March 1976, set out terms which it considered essential for a settlement. Of these, the principles of majority rule and elections between eighteen months and two years were paramount.

In his new role, Ramphal had to deal with a British Government which was still trying to bring about a solution in conjunction with the United States as well as with the UN Secretary-General. The attitude of the British Government towards the Commonwealth was one of measured disdain. Although the main protagonists in the matter were all Commonwealth members, the British Government was not hesitant in showing its preference for working with the United States rather than through the Commonwealth. In 1976, US Secretary of State Henry Kissinger announced his support for the British terms for a settlement; in close collaboration with the British Government, Kissinger initiated a diplomatic campaign and shuttled his way around Africa visiting seven capitals between 25 April and May 2. It was no secret that, like Britain, the US Government still continued to support fully the apartheid government in South Africa, seen as a bastion against communism in Africa.

As a result of these initiatives, Britain convened a diplomatic conference in Geneva on 28 October, chaired by Ivor Richard, the UK Permanent Representative at the United Nations. The Secretariat had observer status, and provided support and advice to the representatives of the liberation movements. The conference broke down again on the question of who should wield political power during any interim period leading to independence. Intensive diplomatic meetings continued as Britain tried to reconvene the conference with ministers, including the new Foreign Secretary David Owen, travelling to Africa with US Secretary of State Cyrus Vance, in the vain hope of getting agreement for a constitutional conference.

Ramphal had to reiterate constantly the Commonwealth's position, which was support for NIBMAR -No Independence Before Majority African Rule. Throughout this period he mobilised the resources and expertise available in the Secretariat. He decided that the Secretariat's contribution should be substantial and one of his first acts was to provide a team of six experts for each nationalist delegation at the Geneva conference. Ramphal sent his then Assistant Secretary-General, Emeka Anyaoku, to Geneva throughout the three months of the conference, assisting the African delegations in every possible way.

The 1977 meeting of Commonwealth leaders was held in London in an atmosphere which could only be described as feverish. All the efforts of leading players in the search to find a solution – Britain, the United States, front-line states leaders, had been broken by Ian Smith's intransigence. Adding to the general disarray was the looming threat that Idi Amin, the much reviled dictator who had terrorised Uganda for many years, was planning to attend. Amin announced that he was coming to London to see Queen Elizabeth II, his Commander-in-Chief as he termed her, and that he would be bringing a troupe of pygmy dancers with him. His murderous regime had been widely publicised worldwide, giving comfort to those who were convinced that African rule should never be permitted in countries with large white minorities.

Ramphal realised that he had to head off this threat, and in mid-1977, flew to Kampala to take the measure of the man and to suggest to Amin that it would be in everybody's best interest for him to stay away. He was successful in this delicate diplomatic exercise and saved the Commonwealth from the ridicule which the media would have poured on it. Without this sideshow, the London meeting was deemed to be a success and Ramphal had been tireless in ensuring this. The Commonwealth strengthened its position by getting agreement on a ban of all sporting contacts with South Africa and Rhodesia, which was agreed at the retreat at Gleneagles in Scotland. The Gleneagles Agreement, and the wider sporting boycott of South Africa which it pioneered, was to become a powerful psychological factor in the struggle against apartheid.

The "internal settlement" of 1978 was seen by the Commonwealth as a tactic for buying time and preserving minority rule. This was an agreement between Smith and three black leaders – Bishop Abel Muzorewa, Ndabaningi Sithole and Chief Chirau to provide a Ministerial Council composed of equal numbers of black and white ministers, with general elections to be held before December 1978. The election was held in April 1979 with Muzorewa being sworn in as Prime Minister of the oddly named Zimbabwe-Rhodesia. International opinion was against this settlement which was described by the Committee on Southern Africa as "fraudulent".

The search for a full settlement continued apace – with all the leading players meeting among themselves and putting forward more and more initiatives.. One of the most important of these were the February 1978 talks between the British and American Governments with leaders of the Patriotic Front in Beira; these ended without any agreement and were reconvened in Dar es Salaam in April. Ramphal sent representatives to these talks and also extended financial assistance to enable the nationalist delegations to be supported by expert technical advisers. Ramphal also met with Muzorewa and conveyed to him the anxieties of Commonwealth Governments about the "internal settlement."

The election of Margaret Thatcher in May 1979 marked the beginning of the end for the Rhodesian regime. It was no secret that while the new Prime Minister's sympathies lay with the settlers in Rhodesia and with the apartheid Government in South Africa, she did not wish to have this issue clouding her time in office. She wanted the issues of NIBMAR off the British agenda. She was on record as referring to the representatives of the African people who were fighting to end white rule as "terrorists". Mrs Thatcher was disposed to accept the bogus internal settlement of 1978 agreed between Smith and such internal leaders as Muzorewa. Indeed, she was elected on a manifesto which looked to the "recognition" of the Muzorewa regime. There is no doubt that she presented a new and enormous challenge to the Commonwealth.

The Commonwealth summit in Lusaka in August 1979 took place against this background of crisis. It was a time when military attacks on the frontline states by both Rhodesia and South Africa were frequent and deadly. Lusaka had been bombed and Zambia was feeling the effects of the decade-long struggle. There were frequent cross-border incursions from Rhodesia, and the bombing of Lusaka was interpreted as an attempt by the Rhodesian regime to assassinate Joshua Nkomo whose headquarters were destroyed. The bombing of Lusaka weeks before the leaders were due there led Mrs Thatcher to suggest, while in New Zealand shortly after she was elected, that she was inclined to advise the Queen not to attend the meeting. In this she was fully supported by Prime Minister Robert Muldoon. On the other hand, the Queen was not only monarch of these two countries but of some 14 other Commonwealth countries whose leaders were prepared to encourage her to attend. In the event that was not necessary, as Buckingham Palace announced that the Queen would be attending the Lusaka meeting.

The security of the Queen, who had undertaken a successful tour of several African countries prior to arriving in Lusaka, where she received an ecstatic welcome, as well as the security of the leaders, presented a huge challenge to the Zambians and Ramphal. In a bid to ensure the safety of the visitors, Ramphal met with Nkomo and persuaded him to make a unilateral ceasefire of the guerilla war during the Queen's visit. Muzorewa had no choice but to do likewise, if he was to command British support for the new arrangements in his country.

This situation highlighted the role of the Queen in the Commonwealth. Through this period, the Queen had never given any indication that she was uncomfortable with the action the Commonwealth was taking in response to the crisis in Rhodesia. She was the monarch who had presided over the ending of the old Commonwealth and had warmly welcomed the new leaders into the family. She had attended every Commonwealth summit, where she met every delegation leader and held private discussions with each of them about their countries and matters on the agenda of the meeting. Every leader left their meeting with the Queen marvelling at her knowledge of what was happening in their countries but also at her interest in reaching a solution to the Rhodesian question which would be acceptable to all the parties. The night she arrived in Lusaka, hundreds turned out to welcome her, and the local newspaper wrote that she was the most welcome British visitor. The welcome afforded Mrs Thatcher who arrived later that evening was a telling contrast to the warm-hearted welcome which had been accorded the Queen.

In his capacity as Secretary-General, Ramphal had always kept the Queen fully briefed on developments as they occurred. He ensured that she received a full set of the background documents for each meeting and that her staff were kept fully abreast of the discussions. In all her years on the throne she had never missed a meeting of leaders and, over the course of the years, she had come to know many of them very well indeed.

Ramphal developed a special relationship with the Queen. He valued her role as Head of the Commonwealth; and respected the sense of caring that she brought to it. Time and again in moments of crisis in the Commonwealth he relied on those strengths and was never shy in drawing on them – with proper circumspection. He acknowledged and cultivated the Queen's position in the Commonwealth as one that went beyond that of Queen of Great Britain. And that is how Commonwealth Heads of Government saw her.

By this time there were clear indications that Britain would be seeking to hold a constitutional conference. In her opening address to the conference, Mrs Thatcher declared that Britain's aim would be "to bring Rhodesia to legal independence on a basis which the Commonwealth and the international community as a whole will find acceptable." As Secretary-General, Ramphal could set the agenda for the meeting, and worked out a strategy with President Kaunda to keep discussion and decisions within a small group of leaders. There would be a short discussion on the issue in the executive session on Rhodesia which was fixed for Friday afternoon.

Ramphal was able to structure this debate by inviting President Nyerere to lead it, which as the *Financial Times* of 11 August reported, he did "with calm and penetration and utter credibility." Further discussion would be delayed for Monday, after the Retreat (where leaders were accustomed to meeting without officials). There, Ramphal planned that leaders would have a chance to work out a solution informally among themselves, without speech-making and recriminations. Because of the security situation in Zambia, there was no question of the leaders being taken away from the capital for the entire weekend; but since it was desirable to have those not involved in the close discussions otherwise engaged, a special excursion was arranged for them to Victoria Falls. In fact the announcement was that the leaders would spend Saturday at Victoria Falls; a small group was quietly asked to stay behind.

That small group gathered in Kenneth Kaunda's study to deal with the Rhodesia question. President Kaunda presided over the discussions which included Margaret Thatcher and her Foreign Secretary Lord Carrington, Julius Nyerere of Tanzania, Malcolm Fraser of Australia, Michael Manley of Jamaica, and Major-General H.E.Adefope, the Nigerian Commissioner for External Affairs, representing a country that had nationalised Shell and BP a few days before the meeting, in a protest at British inaction on Rhodesia. They met on Saturday and Sunday, with Ramphal undertaking the role of coordinator and draftsman assisted by the chairman's assistant, Mark Chona. On the Sunday, a commemorative church service was planned for Lusaka Cathedral, while all were invited that night for a barbecue given by Malcolm Fraser at the residence of the Australian High Commissioner in Lusaka.

Ramphal had started the meeting with a draft Heads of Agreement which he kept to himself, but towards which he hoped to steer the discussion. It was his best judgement of what might be attainable. At the appropriate time, he produced his draft around which consensus quickly built. It was to be the Lusaka Accord, providing for the resumption of British responsibility in Rhodesia, an end to hostilities, the holding of a constitutional conference, free and fair elections with Commonwealth involvement, all leading to an independent Zimbabwe. Ramphal and British officials polished the document on Saturday afternoon and a reconvened group approved it on Sunday morning. It would be commended by these key players to the reconvened plenary of all leaders on Monday morning.

It was also agreed that this historic agreement was to be kept secret until it was revealed to the full meeting at the Executive Session on Monday. But the plan was leaked, and by Sunday afternoon reports reached the British delegation that the Australian media had details of the agreement. News of the leak reached Lord Carrington who immediately wrote a note to Mrs Thatcher – who was then at the Cathedral sitting next to Ramphal – telling her of the development and advising her that she could not be held to her prior agreement. Carrington was particularly worried about the effect on the Conservative Party of news of this agreement reaching London from Australia.

Mrs Thatcher passed the note to Ramphal who scribbled on his Order of Service card deploring the leak but strongly advising against her going back on the agreement. She kept her nerve; and in consultation later with President Kaunda as chairman of the conference, Mrs Thatcher accepted Ramphal's proposal to save the Accord by accelerating the timetable for securing the concurrence of the other leaders. The leaders would hold an impromptu meeting at the Australian barbecue, secure agreement and immediately release the Commonwealth Accord. On Ramphal's orchestration of this plan would depend the future of Zimbabwe.

It was a night of high excitement in Lusaka as Secretariat staff rounded up all the journalists accredited to the conference who were off-duty at that time. The Accord was approved by leaders at the barbecue and among its main points was the Commonwealth's welcome of the British Government's indication that they would call a constitutional conference to which all parties would be invited. Significantly, there was a continuing role for the Commonwealth, as there was provision calling for elections under British authority "with Commonwealth observers". The Accord also reiterated Commonwealth support for genuine black majority rule for the people of Zimbabwe.

This agreement led to the Lancaster House conference which was convened in London in September 1979 with Lord Carrington in the chair. Lord Carrington had never shown any enthusiasm for the Commonwealth's activities with regard to Southern Africa, nor

The young Sonny Ramphal

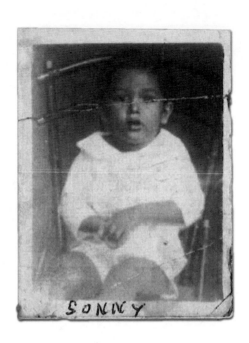

SONNY

Growing up in Georgetown, Guyana

With his father, "J I" in British Guiana. The elder Ramphal was a pioneer educationist remembered notably for helping to change colonial policy which had discriminated against the education of Indian girls

British Guiana's youngest "Silk": Attorney-General Ramphal at 37

Chancellor of Warwick University, with his mother, Grace

Sonny and his wife Lois with their grandchildren, Lucas (front), Sebastian and India (second row), Kira (between her grandparents) and Isaac back row

In celebratory mood after Zimbabwe's independence election: with Prime Minister Robert Mugabe (R) and Sir Lynden Pindling, Prime Minister of the Bahamas (C)

The anti-apartheid struggle – a happy moment among friends. R to L: President Julius Nyerere, Desmond Tutu, Trevor Huddleston and Ramphal

The Commonwealth Eminent Persons Group, in South Africa (top), 1986, with Winnie Mandela R of Malcolm Fraser, former Prime Minister of Australia; and in Marlborough House at the publication of their report, Ramphal with co-chairmen ex-President Obasanjo of Nigeria and Malcolm Fraser

With Fidel Castro at the 2000 South Summit in Havana

On Nelson Mandela's first visit to London after his release from prison, Ramphal gathered Mandela's friends, many of them exiles, to meet him and Mrs Mandela at the Secretary-General's official residence in Mayfair: Huddleston far L, Mrs Ramphal far R

President Mandela, on a UK visit in 1996, is presented with honorary degrees from eight universities at Buckingham Palace and hugs Ramphal, Chancellor of Warwick University

Ramphal sat behind Forbes Burnham, Prime Minister of Guyana (fourth from R, at table) in 1966, at the last Commonwealth Heads of Government Meeting to be held in Marlborough House

In 1971, during a meeting of Commonwealth Caribbean Attorneys-General in Georgetown, Ramphal (second from R), arranged to have them all admitted to Guyana's Inner Bar in a spirit of regionalism

through the three-month conference. The British attitude was summed up by Stephen Chan, Professor of International Relations and Dean of Law and Social Sciences at the School of Oriental and African Studies at the University of London in his recent book: *Robert Mugabe :A life of Power and Violence*. He wrote that at the conference: "the early discernible British attitude was one of tolerance to Nkomo, contempt for Smith, faint contempt but some support for Muzorewa and distrust of Mugabe."

There were also media reports of Carrington's irritation with the activities of Ramphal and the Secretariat. Ironically, this was based on the fact that Ramphal played a pivotal role in ensuring the success of the conference through his close relationships with the leaders of the African Front Line states and with the leaders of the liberation struggle, Joshua Nkomo and Robert Mugabe, as well as with Malcolm Fraser who had good relations with both Thatcher and Carrington. Ramphal's undoubted diplomatic skills, his easy relationships with most of the leaders and his clever handling of the Rhodesian question had enabled him to out-manoeuvre Carrington at Lusaka and for that he was never forgiven. Carrington later said that he would swim the Atlantic to prevent Ramphal from becoming UN Secretary-General, a post for which he was the hot favourite in the early eighties. In his memoirs he mentioned Ramphal only once, in a dismissive way, as someone who had merely interfered in the process.

Ramphal continued to interfere. He maintained daily contacts with the Front-Line leaders and with the Patriotic Front, as the negotiating team of Nkomo and Mugabe was known. He orchestrated sustained Commonwealth diplomatic activities behind the scenes at Marlborough House. Thirty meetings were arranged for Commonwealth representatives to be briefed, many times by representatives of the British Government, on the discussions at Lancaster House. These meetings sometimes convened formally as the Commonwealth Committee on Southern Africa. There were also direct and regular contacts with Commonwealth capitals and with other delegations to the conference and the UN Secretary General.

The Commonwealth was totally committed to a settlement, and Ramphal used his influence to keep the leaders of the Patriotic Front at the conference, despite the pressures they were under to accept a solution that was less than satisfactory. One near breaking point came in November, when Carrington proposed that Rhodesian forces should police the ceasefire. In the end, at the insistence of Ramphal and Kaunda, the PF was able to secure Carrington's agreement to a Commonwealth Monitoring Force.

During the three months of these negotiations, Ramphal was tireless in keeping the Commonwealth's interest in the forefront of public knowledge and understanding. He spoke frequently of his belief that land was the basis for the problems in Rhodesia and had to be the basis of any settlement. He said that he always bore in mind the fact that 80 per cent of the arable land was owned by 5 per cent of the population. Land was a major stumbling block at the Lancaster House conference and there were times when Mugabe and Nkomo threatened to leave unless they were given an assurance that they would be helped to pay compensation for any land distribution which was inevitable.

In order to help keep the negotiations on track, Ramphal had approached the United States, through Kingman Brewster, its Ambassador in London. He wanted to see if the US would be willing to contribute to a fund which would ease the impasse over the land. The response from the US was that it would contribute to an agricultural development fund which could be used to defray any compensation that the constitution required. This was conveyed to the British Government and to the Patriotic Front. There is no reason to doubt that both Mugabe and Nkomo expected that financial help would be forthcoming, to assist in ending the historic injustice, which had left the African people landless in their own country.

In fact, on October 18, Joshua Nkomo after a meeting the previous evening with the British delegation, issued a statement on behalf of the Patriotic Front which stated: "When the conference adjourned we stated that we required clarification on the fund relating to the land question to which the chairman had made reference. We have now obtained assurances that depending on the successful outcome of the conference, Britain, the United States of America and other countries will participate in a multinational financial donor effort to assist in land, agricultural and economic development programmes.

These assurances go a long way in allaying the great concern we have over the whole land question, arising from the great need our people have for land and our commitment to satisfying that need when in Government...."

But a real battle to keep the Commonwealth involved in the final denouement of the Rhodesian question was being played out nightly at Marlborough House. The Lusaka Accord had accepted that independence based on majority rule required a government that was chosen through free and fair elections, properly supervised by the British Government but observed by the Commonwealth.

As the negotiations drew to an end, the representative of the British Government, told the regular meeting of Commonwealth representatives that invitations to observe the elections had been sent to selected Commonwealth Governments and that Canada, Australia, New Zealand and a small Caribbean country had accepted. Tempers flared at that meeting and Ramphal, fully supported by the majority of Commonwealth representatives present, made it clear that the Lusaka Accord had provided for 'Commonwealth' observation of the elections, and that without this process the elections could not be declared valid. He argued: 'It was my understanding that what was envisaged at Lusaka was a collective role for "Commonwealth Observers" rather than separate roles for "observers from Commonwealth countries"[2]. The British representative hinted that Britain would not contribute to a Commonwealth team, and Nigeria immediately stepped in and pledged enough funds to enable the Secretariat to begin putting together an Observer Group.

On 13 December 1979, Ramphal gave the Commonwealth Observer Group its terms of reference in whose drafting he played a personal role. Its crucial paragraph said "The Group's function will be to ascertain in their impartial judgement, whether, in the context of the Lusaka Accord and the Lancaster House Conference, the elections were free and fair'. Ramphal, as Secretary-General had chosen the observers. It was the Commonwealth, not Britain and Lord Soames, the British appointed governor, which would decide the result.

The rest is history – the Commonwealth was able to send a team to Rhodesia. They played an important role in ensuring that the elections in April 1980, although held under difficult conditions in what was in effect a post-war situation, truly gave all the people of Rhodesia, the first chance in their history to vote for a government of their choice.

The new Prime Minister, Robert Mugabe, invited Ramphal to be an honoured guest at the Independence celebrations and on his arrival in Harare, he was greeted by headlines in the local media welcoming him and naming him as one of the chief architects of the end of racial domination and discrimination in that part of southern Africa.

In order to bring about this successful ending, Ramphal deployed his position as Secretary-General to use the Commonwealth's advantages in summit diplomacy to handle common problems. Ramphal's role behind the scenes during this period has been overshadowed by the self-serving accounts which have been written by many of the protagonists. But his contribution has been widely acknowledged by independent observers from academia and the media.

In his 1984 *Round Table* essay "Three Birds of Different Feathers: The Commonwealth, the Commonwealth Secretariat and the Commonwealth Secretary-General" Stephen Chan wrote that "Ramphal's was an amazing role. Many would attribute to him, rather than Carrington, the most important single role in the Zimbabwe episode." Equally important were the roles played by the leaders of the Front Line States, who have also been airbrushed from Anglocentric accounts of the history of this period. It has also been noted that "Due credit for achievements must go both to individual Commonwealth Governments and the Secretariat because the whole process of Commonwealth multilateral diplomacy is the result of the interaction of these two actors"[3].

In an analysis of the Commonwealth's role, Mathew Neuhaus avers that: "Ramphal behind the scenes felt compelled to play an active role of 'behind the scenes broker' in order to keep the British honest to their agreement. Ramphal was also very conscious that the talks were going ahead largely on the basis of credibility given to the Lusaka Agreement by Commonwealth involvement and he needed to defend that credibility. This is borne out by the perceptive comment in the *Scotsman* newspaper noting that the 'Commonwealth is crucial to the London talks. Without Commonwealth agreement, British recognition of the Government in Salisbury would lack credibility'. In doing so, his interventions saved the game for Britain at certain times, particularly near the end when a 'second class' solution might not have been feasible. Indeed at certain times it appeared to be him, not Carrington who was manipulating the parties and the issues."[4]

Ramphal had put much effort into seeing the sun set on Rhodesia and its racist system. The intensity of that struggle enlarges the deep sense of sadness that he now feels about the suffering that Zimbabweans are again made to endure. He has always maintained that a land redistribution scheme was central to the peaceful development of Zimbabwe and he remains disappointed that the promises of the British and US governments to help fund such a scheme were broken. He is disappointed, too, that even in the face of the broken promises by Britain and the US, Mugabe did not fulfill the opportunity that the Commonwealth helped to put in his grasp; the opportunity to show the world that Zimbabwe could be governed democratically for the benefit of all its people.

Why was Shridath Ramphal so resolute in his stand against Smith's Rhodesia and for an independent Zimbabwe? In part, it was in his character to be passionate about the causes he eschewed; but it was more than that. He saw his role as Secretary-General as a kind of stewardship through which the Commonwealth must be helped to live up to its highest ideals. Southern Africa threw down the gauntlet to those ideals. He never believed he was there merely to organise meetings and keep the minutes. He would be betraying the trust Commonwealth leaders reposed in him if he flinched under pressure from pushing the Commonwealth the extra mile toward its deepest commitments. But, as he sometime said to colleagues: "If the Secretariat was always faithful to principle it could not be false to the Commonwealth's highest purposes and would in the end have the support of its Commonwealth constituents."

He is truly a global person. He saw the Commonwealth as being in the service of a wider humanity; and he believed that in some areas – like Rhodesia and South Africa – the Commonwealth had special capacities and competences to bring to the resolution of global problems. It was his duty to make that contribution. On both Rhodesia and, later on, the struggle against apartheid in South Africa he was absolutely right. The Commonwealth's standing rose in the world during his stewardship.

That some of the best people in the Commonwealth wished to join his team at the Secretariat was confirmation to him that the Commonwealth was going the right way. As in Rhodesia, that buoyed him up against opposition which he recognised as an occupational hazard, and sometimes, a badge of distinction.

1   *The Past is Another Country: Rhodesia 1800-1979* by Martin Meredith, Deutsch, 1980, Page 84.

2   Shridath Ramphal's Statement at the Commonwealth Committee on Southern Africa, 23rd November 1979

3   A N Papadopoulos, *Multilateral Diplomacy Within the Commonwealth* Martimus Nijhoff, The Hague 192 P 1352

4   M E K Neuhaus, *The Commonwealth in Contemporary Crises: Britain and the Commonwealth with Special Reference to Rhodesia*, Chapters 2 and 3.

Stitches in Times – Biography of Arnold Smith by Clyde Sanger

Reports of Commonwealth Secretaries-General 1975-1981

The Road to Zimbabwe by Anthony Verrier

Mugabe – A Life of Power and Violence by Stephen Chan

One World To Share – Selected Speeches by Shridath Ramphal

Shridath Ramphal, and his struggle for peaceful change in South Africa

S.K. Rao

Now that South Africa is liberated, it is difficult to remember how difficult it all seemed, in the dark days of apartheid, to see light at the end of the tunnel. It almost seemed beyond one's imagination. The United States and other powers caught in a Cold War found their own logic for continuing to support the status quo, though they were opposed to the travesty that apartheid was. The racist regime of South Africa became an important pillar in the power game between the West and the East. The ethnic links between Europe and the white people of South Africa became another obstacle to change.

The ordinary and decent people in all parts of the world found this intolerable. The leaders of the countries that were freshly liberated from colonial rule, such as India, Ghana, Tanzania, Nigeria, Jamaica and many others could easily emphathise with the suffering of the South Africans. The more perceptive in all parts of the world could see that apartheid represented a violation of the human spirit, in the same way that slavery did. Apartheid questioned the oneness of humanity. And Shridath Ramphal was one of those who saw it. He worked hard, and with imagination, to bring about change in Southern Africa – change that was neither easy to achieve, nor predictable. Yet his individual contribution was great, and in this small contribution of mine I want to trace and reflect on that contribution, as a tribute to him as one of the great human beings of our times.

S. K. Rao, now Director-General of the Administrative Staff College of India, worked at the Commonwealth Secretariat between 1978 and 2001, on tasks which included assisting the Eminent Persons Group and the Commonwealth Committee of Foreign Ministers on Southern Africa.

By the time Shridath Ramphal took the reins at the Commonwealth in 1975 the Commonwealth had already been engaged in pressurising for change in South Africa. The newly liberated countries of the British empire, that had assumed an equal position in the councils of the association, found it unacceptable that a racist regime, capable of inflicting the Sharpeville massacre, sat amidst them. Hence South Africa was allowed to leave the Commonwealth in 1961. But beyond that, despite some UN embargoes on the export of arms to South Africa, adoption of cultural sanctions like the sports boycotts, civil society protests against the racist regime in various forms including voluntary sanctions, and calls by the Heads of Government of the Commonwealth for change, little happened to propel South Africa towards real change. Indeed, in many ways apartheid took a harsher form in South Africa. It was not until the question of Rhodesia's independence came up that global attention began to focus on the South African issue again.

Here the Commonwealth, that brought together the white dominions with the former newly independent countries from Asia, Africa, the Caribbean and the Pacific, provided an excellent, unrivalled forum for pursuing a global agenda, untrammeled by rigid rules or procedures. And Shridath Ramphal used it to best effect. When, in the face of Britain's intransigence over Rhodesian independence, Nigeria was threatening to leave the Commonwealth prior to the Lusaka CHOGM in 1979, Shridath Ramphal knew that such an act could lead to an exodus of many other countries from the association – depriving the world of a valuable forum. He was determined to save it by convincing Nigeria and others to stay in the fold. The Lancaster House Conference of 1979, itself preceded by several meetings, was the result of his determined diplomacy, involving among others President Jimmy Carter of the US. It facilitated a peaceful transition in Rhodesia, in which the Commonwealth, under Shridath Ramphal's leadership, was acknowledged to have played a significant role.

The success of the Commonwealth in bringing about a peaceful change in Rhodesia opened the way to addressing the more difficult issue: how to facilitate a peaceful change in South Africa? As noted earlier, the sanctions then in force, including the Gleneagles Agreement of 1977 discouraging sporting contacts with South Africa – adopted by the Commonwealth soon after Shridath Ramphal became Secretary-General – were not inducing change in South Africa. Britain, under Mrs Thatcher's Prime Ministership, was not willing to see fresh pressures brought on South Africa. But feeling in the rest of the Commonwealth – and within the enlightened parts of Britain and elsewhere – led to fresh consultations. There was a determination that the Commonwealth could not stand by any longer. Shridath Ramphal, sensing this mood, initiated work in the Commonwealth Secretariat on sanctions against South Africa. It was part of his preparation for the 1985 Commonwealth Heads of Government Meeting in the Bahamas.

In 1985 CHOGM in the Bahamas proved to be a watershed in the Commonwealth's role in bringing change to South Africa. Backed by much technical work at the Secretariat on sanctions, and consultations with Heads of Government prior to the meeting, Shridath Ramphal made sanctions the major theme of discussion at the Retreat of Commonwealth Heads in Lyford Cay. Leaders who participated included Bob Hawke of Australia, Quett Masire of Botswana, Margaret Thatcher of Britain, Brian Mulroney of Canada, Rajiv Gandhi of India, Edward Seaga of Jamaica, Moshoeshoe II of Lesotho, Mahathir Mohammad of Malaysia, David Lange of New Zealand, Dlamini of Swaziland, Salim A. Salim of Tanzania, Kenneth Kaunda of Zambia, as well as Ramphal himself. Ramphal, with the help of Rajiv Gandhi and others, played a critical role at Lyford Cay in building a consensus on the way forward. This was despite Mrs Thatcher's unwillingness to join the others in imposing sanctions in any large measure. Perhaps for the first time in the Commonwealth's history, Britain was isolated from all three of the other white dominions, namely, Australia, Canada and New Zealand. This marked a historic break in the evolution of the Commonwealth on a matter of global significance.

The statement issued by the Heads of Commonwealth Governments, including Mrs Thatcher, The Commonwealth Accord on Southern Africa, proved seminal. It called for the immediate and unconditional release of Nelson Mandela and other political prisoners, termination of the existing state of emergency, and initiation of a process of dialogue in the context of a suspension of violence on all sides – including from the government of South Africa. This was a major step forward. It also established a small group of eminent

Commonwealth persons "to encourage through all practicable ways the evolution of that necessary process of political dialogue."

The Eminent Persons Group – or, EPG, as it came to be known – comprised Mr Malcolm Fraser from Australia (Co-chairman), Lord Barber from Britain, Dame Nita Barrow from the Bahamas, Rev Edward Walter Scott from Canada, Sardar Swaran Singh from India, General Olusegun Obasanjo from Nigeria (Co-chairman) and Mr John Malacela from Tanzania, who were nominated by their respective governments. The strong membership clearly indicated the weight of the Commonwealth behind the mission. The task of the EPG was to advance the process of change in South Africa, by all practicable means. The appointment of this group – and the manner in which it worked – heralded much hope. And indeed it did create a momentum by meeting leaders from all sides including members of the South African cabinet, Nelson Mandela, Desmond Tutu, Allan Boesak, and representatives of various other groups and people. In the light of its conversations, and committed to promoting dialogue for peaceful change in South Africa, the EPG developed a "negotiating concept." This set out the measures needed to create a climate of confidence, and enable all concerned to turn to the task of constructing a new South Africa. Measures to be taken by the government of South Africa included removal of the military from the townships, and the release of Nelson Mandela and other prisoners; measures by the ANC and others included entering into negotiations and suspending violence.

The work of the EPG had indeed aroused much hope. I remember Shridath Ramphal meeting leaders such as Kenneth Kaunda and Robert Mugabe, to discuss bridging the differences between the African National Congress and the South African government over the suspension of violence. Despite the hope placed on the EPG mission, however, it ended in failure. The government of South Africa made a calculated assault on Botswana, Zambia and Zimbabwe on 19 May 1986, with the clear intent of nullifying the peace process. It was clear to all that the apartheid government of South Africa refused to take the opportunity opened up by the EPG for peaceful change.

In the face of this failure, the challenge confronting the Commonwealth was either to conclude that peaceful change was not possible, and leave the matter for resolution to other means beyond its remit, or to persist in efforts for peaceful change. The Eminent Persons Group had itself debated the issue, and expressed the belief that "sanctions remain the most effective peaceful path to the ending of apartheid." The Commonwealth opted to accept this, and turned to intensify sanctions. As Shridath Ramphal says in his Foreword to the EPG Mission Report[1] "Sanctions and peace for South Africa have now become one and the same." (p14). This decision was influenced by the view of the EPG that the absence of real economic pressure on the government – and its belief that it may never have to face such pressure – were helping to defer any change.

Hence, as envisaged in the Nassau *Commonwealth Accord on Southern Africa*, sanctions became the focus of subsequent Commonwealth action. The seven Commonwealth Heads of Government comprising the EPG countries, who met in London in August 1986, considered the adoption of further sanctions; and with the exception of Britain, adopted a package of measures that included a ban on air links with South Africa, and other trade and financial sanctions such as a ban on all new bank loans, and withdrawal of consular facilities.

The British government, while not agreeing to the full range of sanctions agreed by the other leaders, had agreed to impose voluntary bans on new investment and promotion of tourism; it also agreed to implement any EEC decisions on trade sanctions.

The EPG Mission and the London summit of the seven Commonwealth Heads of Government had thus profoundly changed the tone of international engagement with South Africa. By these actions, the Commonwealth had shown that it did not agree with the argument put forward by those – including some from outside South Africa – who maintained that sanctions would hurt the black South Africans. As Shridath Ramphal says in his Foreword to the EPG Mission Report:

> "Ordinary black people throughout South Africa look to the world for more than just moral clarity. Those outside who say that sanctions will 'hurt the blacks' do not know how intense black suffering already is. It is, in any case, they [the outsiders] have no right to make a judgment, when the blacks themselves see

sanctions, and any additional suffering these involve, as preferable to the far greater tragedy they would otherwise face." (p15)

The stand taken by the Commonwealth following the EPG Mission Report in June 1986 had a profound impact on the global understanding of what was holding back progress in South Africa. The Commonwealth sanctions were followed by the United States Congress. Congress adopted a Comprehensive Anti-Apartheid Act in September 1986 over President Reagan's veto, signaling a further isolation of South Africa. This action by the US, a superpower and considered a strategic ally of South Africa, had a profound effect on the global community's understanding of the extent to which apartheid South Africa could carry on as usual. These steps by the Commonwealth and the US were in turn followed by an intensification of measures in Europe and elsewhere.

The Commonwealth Heads of Government, meeting a year later in Canada in October 1987, decided that the failure of the EPG Mission to bring the South African Government to the negotiating table should not take it off the agenda of the world community. With the exception of Britain, they decided to establish a Committee of Foreign Ministers (CFMSA), comprising Australia, Canada, Guyana, India, Nigeria, Tanzania, Zambia and Zimbabwe, with the Foreign Minister of Canada, Joe Clark, chairing it. This was again a brilliant step on the part of the Commonwealth, which brought the old white dominions of the Commonwealth away from Britain. The purpose of the CFMSA was to provide a high level impetus to the furtherance of change in South Africa. In establishing the CFMSA, an objective of the Commonwealth leaders was to see that the wider, tighter and more intensified application of economic and other sanctions must remain an essential part of the international community's response to apartheid. It wanted a more concerted application of the global sanctions programme.

The CFMSA, which met every six months until after the release of Nelson Mandela, served as a focus for pressure and change in South Africa, and as diplomatic channel for advancing negotiations. One of its early actions was to request the Commonwealth Secretary-General to commission an independent evaluation of the application and impact of sanctions. This was eventually carried out by a group of experts under the leadership of Dr Joseph Hanlon, confirming the legitimacy and effectiveness of sanctions as a policy to induce the dismantling of apartheid.[2]

Meanwhile, there was a growing awareness in the international community of South Africa's vulnerability to financial sanctions, starting with the refusal of international financial institutions in New York and elsewhere in July and August 1985 to roll over the loans that they had lent to various clients in South Africa – both because of the turbulence in South Africa and also because of the resistance by shareholders and the general public against such loans. CFMSA, at the initiative of the Australian Foreign Minister, Mr Gareth Evans, saw this as opening an effective additional avenue for mounting pressure on South Africa, and commissioned a study on financial sanctions, with the support of the Australian Government.[3] These financial sanctions have the merit of being cost-free to governments and, by acting in tune with the instincts of financial markets, they are self-sustaining. The study confirmed that the pressures exerted by churches, anti-apartheid groups and others throughout the world were playing an indispensable part in convincing the South African regime that it was vulnerable to financial sanctions; once in place they could become self-reinforcing through market driven behaviour. The conclusions of the report helped those fighting apartheid to take heart and keep hope alive – at a time when light at the end of the tunnel looked faint. The Commonwealth thus played a vital role in keeping up the pressure for peaceful change in South Africa.

The value of sanctions was stressed as a policy for change, and the Hanlon Report stressed that sanctions were an essential part of the negotiating process, not an alternative to it. But there were some voices who wondered whether it was right to keep up the pressure at a time when Pretoria had entered into negotiations for Namibian independence, and was presenting a softer face to the world. Would not a hardening of sanctions send the wrong signal? In response to this, Shridath Ramphal wrote:

> "Such hesitations ignore the fact that South Africa prognosticated for more than a decade over independence in Namibia and withdrawal from Angola and agreed only when it was under pressure. Peace in Angola and Namibia comes not because of a sudden outbreak of good will in Pretoria. Rather, heavier trade

and financial sanctions, an increasingly effective arms embargo and consequential military reverses, especially at Cuito Cuanavale in Angola, all helped to convince Pretoria that its illegal occupation of Namibia and Angola were unsustainable. It was only the wave of sanctions in 1985 and 1986, led by the Commonwealth, helped by US Congressional action and combined with other internal and international pressure, that jolted Pretoria into a sense that change was becoming unavoidable."[4]

A continuing worry for the Commonwealth was the possible negative fallout of sanctions on South Africa on the neighbouring states – Botswana, Lesotho, Swaziland, Zambia, Zimbabwe and others – whose economies were closely intermeshed with that of South Africa. This was a real concern. As the EPG Report noted, despite the protestations to the contrary, the South African regime not only believed in the power of sanctions, it has consistently applied them on its neighbours!

The Commonwealth had been concerned with the power of South Africa to do damage to its neighbours, and use it as an instrument to stall change. The leaders of the neighbouring front-line states, who were conscious of this threat, continuously stressed their determination to withstand it. They were willing to undergo suffering, if need be, rather than compromise with the evil of apartheid. This was evident in the discussions at the CHOGMs and in the conversations the EPG had with them during their mission.

An aspect of the Commonwealth's response to the vulnerability of the front-line states to South African pressure was not only its determination to stand by them morally, but to look for practical ways to help. An early indication of this was the response by Shridath Ramphal, as early as 1978, to a request from Botswana, Lesotho and Swaziland and neighbouring states. They asked for a Commonwealth Secretariat team to investigate the feasibility of arrangements by which they could increase cooperation with each other, and reduce dependence on South Africa. Shridath Ramphal sent an exploratory team from the Secretariat to hold conversations with the BLS governments and prepare a report. This was eventually to fructify into the Southern African Development Cooperation Conference

(SADCC), which played an important role in consolidating political and economic cooperation among the front-line states.

The offer of succour and moral support, to the brave stand taken by the front-line states, became an important agenda for the wider Commonwealth, especially in summit discussions. The Commonwealth set up a Mozambique Fund in 1987 to provide technical assistance for the newly independent state, and to show that the Commonwealth leaders stood by her. And, significantly, Commonwealth leaders, at their summit in Vancouver in 1987, declared their readiness to help deal with the security needs of Mozambique. These steps were much valued not only for the provision of the technical assistance, but had the consequence of bringing Mozambique closer to the English-speaking Commonwealth. They led to the admission of Mozambique into the Commonwealth in 1995, following a proposal from Nelson Mandela at the Retreat of Commonwealth Heads in Millbrook in New Zealand in 1995. This act of admission, of a former Portuguese colony, has set a constitutional precedent. The Commonwealth now has a larger role, helping like-minded countries to reach out to each other on the basis of affinity, rather than historic empire-based relationships.

After three significant terms as Commonwealth Secretary-General, Shridath Ramphal left office in the first half of 1990. Commonwealth Heads had elected Chief Emeka Anyaoku to succeed him at their summit in 1989 in Kuala Lumpur. But, by the time Shridath Ramphal left the Secretariat, he had the satisfaction of seeing Nelson Mandela released from prison. It was an event that brought tears of joy to all those who had watched an event that was broadcast throughout the world. And Ramphal himself had the pleasure of receiving Mandela at his official residence at 40B Hill Street, Mayfair, within months of his release from prison. It was a moment of great delight for someone who believed in the oneness of humanity, who had led an incessant struggle against the evil of apartheid. He led this struggle with political acumen, finding strength in the multiracial nature of the Commonwealth, and with commitment to peace. Humanity owes much to him.

— ∞ —

1   *Mission to South Africa: The Commonwealth Report*, Penguin, London, 1986

2   *South Africa: The Sanctions Report*, Penguin Books in association with James Currrey, London 1989

3   This was published eventually. See Keith Ovenden and Tony Cole, *Apartheid and international Finance*, Penguin Books, 1989.

4   Foreword, p xii, in *South Africa: The Sanctions Report*, Penguin Books in association with James Currey, London, 1989.

Ramphal and the Caribbean

— ∞ —

Ramphal, the US-led invasion of Grenada, and the Commonwealth

Ronald Sanders

— ∞ —

Before he entered Marlborough House in London as Commonwealth Secretary-General, Sonny Ramphal had been an architect of Caribbean regional integration and an ardent advocate of genuine non-alignment in the external affairs of the area.

When he received information in London in October 1983 that several Caribbean countries were seriously contemplating inviting the United States of America to invade the tiny island of Grenada to overthrow a military government that had seized power in a bloody coup d'etat, he was deeply troubled.

This would have been bad news for any Secretary-General, but it was particularly troubling to Ramphal because this was his region. All eyes would be upon him to judge how he treated it. But beyond his personal concerns, he recognised that the invitation to the US by some Commonwealth Caribbean countries to invade Grenada would create deep division within both the Caribbean and the Commonwealth.

He also had a wider concern. At stake was the principle of non-intervention in the internal affairs of states which had long been a cornerstone of international law, and which was enshrined in the Charter of the United Nations.

The violation of this fundamental principle posed enormous problems to global stability and the rule of law internationally – a development which ran counter to Ramphal's deeply held commitment to the

— ∞ —

Sir Ronald Sanders, is an international affairs consultant and commentator on Caribbean affairs. He has published widely on small states and was formerly High Commissioner for Antigua and Barbuda in the United Kingdom.

supremacy of international law. He was right to be concerned, for within two decades the US government under George W Bush would elevate the decision to invade Grenada to justify his policy of pre-emption, in the invasions first of Afghanistan and then Iraq.

Incidentally, this language of "pre-emption" was first used by members of the Organisation of Eastern Caribbean States (OECS)[1] which, ostensibly, issued the first invitation to the US to lead the invasion. In a message on the day of the invasion, sent by the OECS Secretariat on behalf of its member states, to Ramphal in his capacity as Commonwealth Secretary-General, the OECS Secretariat declared:

> "Three governments have responded to the OECS member governments' request to form a multinational force for the purpose of undertaking a pre-emptive defensive strike in order to remove this dangerous threat to peace and security in the sub region".[2]

From London, Ramphal tried his best to follow events in a Caribbean that was in turmoil. A few days before, on 19 October, soldiers under the command of General Hudson Austin had executed the Prime Minister, Maurice Bishop, three ministers of the government and two trade union leaders. Several other supporters of Bishop had been pushed over a precipice to their death.

The Caribbean image, as an idyll of tranquillity, was shattered overnight.

Matters worsened the following day when Austin, the commanding general of Grenada's "People's Revolutionary Army", announced the formation of a Revolutionary Military Council and imposed a shoot-on-sight curfew.

Ramphal "unreservedly" condemned these events at once.

Bishop himself had come to power by a coup d'etat in 1979 – albeit a bloodless one. But, he had set in train what Ramphal described as "a chain of tragedy that begins with the overthrow of constitutional government, and the deep passions and anxieties that are aroused when the contests of super-powers are brought within regions of small developing countries".[3]

Having overthrown the unpopular government of Sir Eric Gairy on 13 March 1979, Bishop and his lieutenants – in particular Bernard Coard, his deputy prime minister – declined to hold elections to restore a constitutional government. Ramphal had immediately visited Grenada and secured Bishop's agreement to his establishment (as Commonwealth Secretary General) of a special Caribbean Advisory Group which included the distinguished jurist from Dominica, Telford Georges, and William Demas then still President of the Caribbean Development Bank. Coard had only reluctantly concurred in this and was rigidly opposed to the group's insistent advice to Bishop that parliamentary elections be held. The group's advice reflected the urgings of the governments of Grenada's closest neighbouring countries, the members of the OECS and Barbados.[4] The Coard view prevailed and instead, the Bishop government drew Grenada close to Cuba and the Soviet Union causing even further disquiet among the governments of the OECS, Barbados and, increasingly, the United States.

But, it should be noted that, as admitted by the British Foreign and Commonwealth Office (FCO), Britain – the traditional ally and aid donor to Grenada – "did not sufficiently recognise the need for positive policies to provide an antidote to Cuban and Soviet influence on the island".[5] And, the government of the United States was downright hostile, cutting-off all bilateral aid to the country and even refusing to allow its contributions to the Caribbean Development Bank to be made available to Grenada.

The US government judged the Bishop government to be in the Cuban-Soviet axis, and presumably to be an enemy of the United States. Among the reasons the US cited for its assessment of the Bishop regime were:

- In the United Nations, Grenada voted with the Soviets and their allies in over 92 per cent of the votes of the 1982 general assembly – a pro-Soviet record exceeding even that of Nicaragua;

- The bulk of the financing (for a new airport in Grenada) came from Cuba, which was providing services valued at $40 million, supplemented by $2 million from Syria, $2 million from Iraq, $6 million from Libya, and $2 million from Algeria. Construction was in the hands of Cuban workers with arms and the training to use them.[6]

Seven months before the US-led invasion, the US President, Ronald Reagan, had already set the stage for it. In a speech to the National Association of Manufacturers, he said "that tiny little island is building now, or having built for it, on its soil and shores, a naval base, a superior air base, storage bases and facilities for the storage of munitions, barracks, and training grounds for the military. I'm sure all of that is not simply to encourage the export of nutmeg."

And, he declared: "It isn't nutmeg that's at stake in the Caribbean and Central America; it is the United States national security". Stating that "Soviet military theorists want to destroy our capacity to re-supply Western Europe in case of an emergency", he said: "We've been slow to understand that the defence of the Caribbean and Central America against Marxist-Leninist takeover is vital to our national security in ways we're not accustomed to thinking about".[7]

Two years before, in 1981, the elements of Reagan's policy toward Grenada were being informed by a Caribbean leader – Edward Seaga, the Prime Minister of Jamaica. Shortly after he took up residence at the White House in January 1981, Reagan's first foreign visitor was Seaga who had himself been elected to lead a Jamaican government three months before.

In his election campaign, Seaga had pledged to break diplomatic relations with Cuba and to draw Jamaica close to the United States – direct reversals of the policies pursued by the socialist Michael Manley who had been in charge of the country's affairs for the previous decade. True to his word, Seaga broke diplomatic relations with Cuba and established close relations with insiders in the Reagan camp who were later to become key players not only in the Reagan government, but later in the administration of George W Bush – among them were Richard Perle and Paul Wolfowitz, two of the architects of Bush's policy of unilateralism and his doctrine of pre-emption: they wanted to strike enemies of the US in anticipation of anti-US activity.

Seaga had come to office at a time when the Caribbean's links were divided between the United States and the Soviet Union. Prior to his becoming Prime Minister, Jamaica along with Guyana led by Forbes Burnham, and Grenada under the Maurice Bishop regime were the closest allies of Cuba in a Cold War context. The remaining members of the OECS countries and Barbados continued to be strongly linked to the US while Trinidad and Tobago, under Dr Eric Williams, stood aloof from ties to either side. The Bahamas, led by Sir Lynden Pindling, was literally on America's doorstep and while Pindling would do nothing to offend the US, he was anxious not to encourage its undue influence. Belize – the other member of the Caribbean Community and Common Market (CARICOM) at the time – was under threat from Guatemala, which claimed all of Belizean territory. Never certain about whom the US would support in the Belize-Guatemala dispute, the Belizean leader, George Price, was also wary of the Americans.

In the event, in 1982, as the Seaga and Reagan administrations grew close and worked together in the Caribbean, the Heads of Government of CARICOM, which had been formed in 1973 to deepen integration amongst the participating Caribbean countries, had not met together for eight years. A quarrel between Williams, Burnham and Manley had created the hiatus which finally ended in 1982 when Williams died and was replaced by George Chambers as Prime Minister of Trinidad and Tobago.

As part of his policy in the Caribbean of closer links with the US and greater distance from the Soviet Union, Seaga had been promoting the heretical idea of the creation of "CARICOM 2" a new entity to replace the existing CARICOM, but one that would exclude Guyana and Grenada from its membership – the two countries whose governments had the closest links to Cuba and the Soviet Union. J M G "Tom" Adams, the Prime Minister of Barbados, was Seaga's closest ally in this cause, though it is likely that others such as the Prime Ministers of Dominica and St Lucia, Eugenia Charles and John Compton, were also supportive.

In the end, the attempt to create CARICOM 2 came to nothing because of a lack of majority support among the governments of CARICOM. Antigua and Barbuda's Prime Minister, Vere Cornwall Bird Snr, even though an ally of the US, was strongly against any move to fragment CARICOM. In 1982, he promoted the resumption of meetings of CARICOM Heads of Government and proposed Antigua as the venue, but conceded to Jamaica when he learned that Seaga was keen to host it.

The conference was chaired by Seaga and was attended by the Heads of Government of every CARICOM country including on the one hand, Burnham and Bishop, and on the other Adams, Charles, and Compton.

Two results of the conference are significant.

First, in the Ocho Rios Declaration the Heads asserted that "while recognising that the emergence of ideological pluralism in the Community responds to internal processes and is an irreversible trend within the international system, we are committed to ensuring that it will not inhibit the processes of integration." On the face of it, this seemed to have accepted that individual countries of CARICOM could pursue relations with the US or the Soviet Union as they saw fit. But, indeed, Seaga, Adams, Charles and Compton remained unhappy particularly with Grenada.

Second, the conference "considered that the international system was increasingly characterised by the use of force... and by the assertion by the great powers of spheres of interest", and it "affirmed the inadmissibility of... interference in the internal affairs of States."[8] As the subsequent invasion of Grenada by the US with the active participation of Jamaica, Barbados and the members of the OECS would clearly demonstrate, the affirmation of the inadmissibility of interference in the internal affairs of States was not worth the paper it was written on.

In the wake of the murder of Maurice Bishop and the formation of a military government in Grenada on 20 October, Seaga opened discussions with the Reagan administration about an invasion. His close ally in the enterprise was Tom Adams, the Barbados Prime Minister who invited the governments of the OECS to attend a meeting in Barbados to discuss Grenada.

There is little doubt that the US government wanted to invade Grenada. What they needed was a suitable cover. Therefore, an invitation needed to be contrived. And, it was easy enough to get such an invitation from the members of the OECS, some of whom were genuinely fearful of the example that Grenada would set within their own countries among radical groups with communist links. Many of them had such groups, financed by the Cuban and Libyan regimes, which were active thorns in the sides of the governments. Leaders of these groups, including Maurice Bishop, had met on Union Island in the Grenadines prior to the March 1979 coup d'etat in Grenada, and had declared their intention to remove the governments from office by whatever means necessary.

Some leaders of the OECS, Compton and Charles in particular, regretted that, when the 1979 coup d'état occurred, they could not persuade Britain or the US to invade Grenada. Efforts had been made through the Eastern Caribbean High Commission in London to persuade British Prime Minister Margaret Thatcher to intervene. She declined. Much to the chagrin of Compton especially, attempts to persuade the British government to sever diplomatic relations with Grenada also proved fruitless. The British government argued that Britain recognised states not governments, and since Sir Paul Scoon had been retained as the Governor-General and the representative of the Queen, diplomatic links would continue.

Ramphal's influence in London was not inconsiderable. He strenuously urged continued British government engagement with Grenada.

An uneasy relationship continued between the Bishop government in Grenada and the other governments in the OECS. But, once Bishop was killed and the military government established in October 1983, the members of the OECS were resolved that unconstitutional government should not succeed as an example to ambitious groups within their own countries. If they had the means to enter Grenada and topple the regime they would have done so unhesitatingly. In the face of their own lack of capacity, the option put to them by Seaga and Adams of inviting the US to invade became very attractive.

On 21 October, representatives of the OECS governments met in Barbados with Tom Adams and Edward Seaga. They sought a legitimate basis for inviting the US to invade Grenada and they decided upon Article 8 of the OECS Treaty which provided for collective defence against "external" attack. Present at the meeting at the Dover Convention Centre were representatives of the US military who explained how an invasion could be accomplished.

A meeting of all the CARICOM states was then convened in Trinidad on 22 and 23 October under the chairmanship of George Chambers. It was a rancorous meeting. The Bahamas, Belize, Guyana and Trinidad and Tobago were on one side with the members of the OECS, Barbados and Jamaica on the other. A set of points were discussed which would be put to the military government in Grenada for its agreement. Among them were:

- The immediate establishment of a broad based civilian government of national reconciliation whose composition was acceptable to the Governor-General. The primary function of that government would be the putting into place of arrangements for the holding of elections at the earliest possible date; and

- The acceptance of deployment in Grenada of a Peace-Keeping Force, comprising contingents contributed by CARICOM States.[9]

But, Seaga in particular wanted no such dialogue with the military regime. He was for an invasion by the US and he convinced the leaders of the OECS that such an invasion was possible. When the government representatives left Trinidad on 23 October, they were an utterly divided group. No joint decision had been made on Grenada. Further, they had no idea whether the US would undertake the invasion or not, but troops from Jamaica and some OECS countries had been flown into Barbados to join Barbadian soldiers to await confirmation from the US government that it would lead "Operation Urgent Fury", as the US named the Grenada invasion.

Eugenia Charles, the Dominica Prime Minister and then chairman of the OECS, was awakened in the early morning of 25 October and flown by the US government to Washington to appear on Television with President Reagan to announce that the Grenada invasion was launched that morning. The television announcement was the first inkling that the governments of the OECS countries and other CARICOM countries had that the invasion was on.

Not even Margaret Thatcher, the British Prime Minister, and close friend of Ronald Reagan had been told that the invasion would take place.

On 24 October, as CARICOM leaders were leaving Trinidad at the end of a meeting that left them deeply divided, Reagan wrote to Thatcher saying that "the nations of the OECS have unanimously decided to pursue a collective security effort to restore peace and order in Grenada and have formally requested United States support and participation." He told her that he was "giving serious consideration to the OECS' request", and advised that "they have already assembled forces in Barbados from the various island nations." He concluded by saying that he knew she "would want to be kept informed of any role the United States may decide to play in support of the island nations of the Caribbean" and undertook to inform her "in advance should our forces take part in the proposed collective security force."[10]

Later that same day, Reagan wrote to Thatcher again to say: "I have decided to respond positively to this request (from the OECS to intervene in Grenada). I understand that Barbados and Jamaica have also responded favourably."[11] But, he did not tell her when the operation would take place.

At 12.30am on 25 October, Thatcher sent Reagan the following message:

"This action will be seen as intervention by a Western country in the internal affairs of a small independent nation, however unattractive its regime. I ask you to consider this in the context of our wider East/West relations and of the fact that we will be having in the next few days to present to our Parliament and people the siting of Cruise missiles in this country. I must ask you to think most carefully about these points. I cannot conceal that I am deeply disturbed by your latest communication. You asked for my advice. I have set it out and hope that even at this late stage you will take it into account before events are irrevocable."[12]

By then, the US-led invasion of Grenada was in its final stages of being launched, and it went ahead without the knowledge of the British government.

The next day, 26 October, Reagan called Thatcher to explain that he did not tell her that the invasion was on because there was a security leak on his end; it was a security leak about which he said he was so concerned that "we did not even give a firm answer to the Caribbean States. We told them we were planning, but we were so afraid of this source and what it would do; it could almost abort the mission, with the lives that could have been endangered."[13]

On the day of the invasion and in subsequent media statements, Thatcher and her ministers played aggrieved parties, upset that the US had invaded a Commonwealth country and one of which the Queen was still Head of State. But, the record of Thatcher's conversation with Reagan indicated no such aggravation. The most that could be said of her attitude to Reagan was reflected in her own words to him: "I just hope Ron, that it (the restoration of constitutional government in Grenada) will be very soon and that they will manage to put together a government which can get back to democracy."

Thereafter, it was pleasantries between two good friends:

"President Reagan:
    As I say, I'm sorry for any embarrassment that we caused you, but please understand that it was just our fear of our own weakness over here with regard to secrecy.
Prime Minister Thatcher:
    It was very kind of you to have rung, Ron.
President Reagan:
    Well, my pleasure.
Prime Minister Thatcher:
    I appreciate it. How is Nancy?
President Reagan:
    Just fine.
Prime Minister Thatcher:
    Good. Give her my love.
President Reagan:
    I shall.
Prime Minister Thatcher:
    I must return to this debate in the House. It is a bit tricky.
President Reagan:
    All right. Go get 'em. Eat 'em alive.
Prime Minister Thatcher:
    Good-bye.

On the morning of this conversation between Reagan and Thatcher, Sonny Ramphal was interviewed by the BBC's "Today" programme about the invasion. He was in far more sombre mood than Thatcher. Questioned about whether he was asked for his advice prior to the invasion, he said: "No. I was not. I wish indeed I was. I would not have had any difficulty in saying that there were other ways that must be pursued... that we don't in fact help Grenada or help the Caribbean by taking the law into our own hands, or worse still inviting external powers to take the law into their hands on behalf of the region".[14]

He went on to make it clear that he was against the US invasion. He declared:

> "In the wake of what obviously was a divided region, a divided Caribbean on the question of intervention of any kind, I would have thought that the United States, in this situation, as a friend of the region – and it has been a friend of the region in many respects – would have been counselling calm and wisdom, would have been counselling negotiation, would have been helping the region to put great pressure on the quite grotesque regime that killed Maurice Bishop and seized power, before restoring to this kind of armed intervention."[15]

This was also the morning that he received the telex message from the OECS Secretariat, on behalf of the members of the OECS that they with the US, Jamaica and Barbados had "taken a pre-emptive defensive strike" against the military regime in Grenada.

Within that message was what Ramphal recognised as a possible way to get the US troops out of Grenada and to place authority in Grenada back into Grenadian hands. The OECS Secretariat had stated:

> "It is the intention of the member governments of the OECS that once the threat has been removed, they will invite the Governor-General of Grenada to assume executive authority of the country under the provisions of the Grenada constitution of 1973 and to appoint a broad-based interim government to administer the country pending the holding of general elections."[16]

Ramphal said on the same day: "Nothing must obscure the urgent need to provide the people of Grenada with the earliest possible opportunity to determine their own future free of pressures or constraints of any kind. There may be a role for the Commonwealth to play in contributing to the restoration of democracy."[17]

Seized with the notions of constitutionality and an interim administration, he immediately began to work on assembling such an administration. Concurrently, he sought to put together eminent constitutional lawyers, well known to the Caribbean, who could advise the Governor-General, Sir Paul Scoon.

In the aftermath of the invasion, the US secured from Scoon a letter dated prior to the invasion inviting them to participate. There has always been much speculation about whether the letter was signed and backdated by Scoon. Two things are known for sure. First, at no time prior to the invasion did anyone say that such an invitation had been received. Reagan certainly did not mention it to Thatcher in his letters to her of 24 October or in their telephone conversation of 26 October. Second, after the invasion the US justified the invasion on the basis that: "The Governor-General's appeal carried exceptional moral and legal weight because it came from the sole remaining source of governmental legitimacy in Grenada. An invitation by lawful government authority is a valid legal basis for foreign states to provide the requested assistance."[18] In other words, notwithstanding the earlier invitation from the members of the OECS, the US needed the invitation from Scoon to give their invasion some modicum of legitimacy.

In the event, Scoon was given executive authority of a Grenada occupied by US troops whose command was calling the shots. In Ramphal's mind an interim administration of Grenadians and the withdrawal of US troops became the priorities.

In the following days, while Grenada became the hot issue in the Security Council of the United Nations, Ramphal set about identifying persons who could form an interim administration, and others who could provide constitutional advice. His focus was to put Grenada in Grenadian hands, get US troops out and replace them with a Caribbean police force until general elections could be held to elect a government.

As early as 28 October, Ramphal had engaged Scoon in discussion. Ramphal's note of the conversation indicated that, at the time, Scoon was keen to get qualified Grenadians to constitute a caretaker government. He specifically identified Alister McIntyre, a distinguished Grenadian economist who was then Deputy Secretary-General of the UN Conference on Trade and Development (UNCTAD) and a former Secretary-General of CARICOM, and Nicholas Braithwaite, a Grenadian based in Guyana as Head of the Commonwealth Youth

Programme in the Caribbean. Ramphal concurred in the choice of both men and undertook to pursue the matter with them.[19]

Ramphal spoke to McIntyre the same day and got a positive response on the condition that "he (McIntyre) would expect the withdrawal of American forces and their replacement by an appropriate security unit drawn from a broad band of Commonwealth countries including all Caribbean countries."[20]

On the following day, Ramphal confirmed to Scoon the readiness of both McIntyre and Braithwaite to serve and the Commonwealth Secretariat's willingness to facilitate their service. With regard to McIntyre's condition that American forces would be withdrawn to be replaced by Commonwealth security, Scoon confirmed that "this was his thinking also and he would want to discuss the question fully with Alister, principally in terms of timing which was inevitably responsive to the existing situation."[21]

As it turned out, Scoon eventually rejected the idea of a withdrawal of US troops, and Alister McIntyre could not take up the task for reasons of ill-health. But, Ramphal had laid the foundation with Scoon – and, behind the scenes, with Seaga and the leaders of the OECS through Tom Adams – for an interim administration whose priority task would be the holding of general elections.

Ramphal also knew that the fireworks that had occurred at the UN and other UN bodies were clearly a rehearsal for the drama that could be expected to play out in India a month later, when Commonwealth Heads of Government would meet from 23 to 29 November.

The US was forced to use its veto in the Security Council on 28 October to avoid being declared a flagrant violator of international law. But, it could not save itself from the consequences of a debate in the General Assembly in which 108 countries voted on 2 November for a resolution that deplored the invasion as a flagrant violation of international law, called for the immediate cessation of armed intervention and the immediate withdrawal of foreign troops. Only nine countries voted against the resolution – the US, its six Caribbean partners in the invasion, Israel and El Salvador.

Commonwealth African and Asian countries were especially vocal in condemning the invasion of a Commonwealth country, and they were concerned, if not angry, about the participation of Commonwealth Caribbean countries in giving the US cover in the affair. Ramphal knew that confrontation was coming at the summit conference in India.

He had a two-fold task. The first was to ensure that Commonwealth Caribbean participation with the US in the invasion of Grenada did not fracture the Commonwealth; the second was to rebuild a relationship among the Heads of Commonwealth Caribbean governments who had not met since their stormy meeting in Trinidad on the day before the invasion, and who remained divided in the pro and anti invasion camps.

Grenada was not on the agenda of the Commonwealth conference as representatives of 41 countries met in New Delhi under the chairmanship of India's Prime Minister, Indira Gandhi. The first day of the meeting went by with no reference to Grenada except for a brief but biting comment by Gandhi in her statement at the opening ceremony. It was a comment directed as much to the Caribbean countries that had participated in the invasion as it was to the US. She said:

"In the wider interest of peace, all powers should accept and strictly observe the principles of peaceful coexistence, non-intervention and non-interference. We cannot acquiesce in the reasons being advanced to justify the use of force by one state against another, to install regimes of particular persuasion or to destabilise regimes deemed to be inconvenient. Recent unfortunate events in Grenada have caused profound disquiet."[22]

The first day and the morning of the second were taken up by a lengthy discussion on East/West relations and the question of disarmament under the broad brush of "The World Political Scene: Global Trends and Prospects". Then, close to mid-day on the second day, the seething anger of the African countries was unleashed over what they considered to be the cover that Caribbean countries had given to the US to invade Grenada.

First, Zambia's President Kenneth Kaunda and then Robert Mugabe of Zimbabwe spoke to the issue. They both claimed that a precedent had been set for powerful neighbours such as South Africa (still then under the apartheid regime) to invade them. Kaunda declared that "those of his colleagues in the Caribbean who had acted with the United States had created a real nightmare for him personally and for his country."[23] Mugabe was even more direct. He stated: "If their colleagues in the Commonwealth could sanction this kind of thinking by sanctioning the invasion of Grenada, the African member states were entitled to regard them as acting against African interests."[24] Later in the debate, Tanzania's President, Julius Nyerere, practically accused the leaders of the Caribbean countries that participated in the invasion of lying. He said "it was in the nature of man to try to justify and find good reasons for what he had done. Those in the Eastern Caribbean had given their good reasons for joining the Americans in the invasion. Frankly, he thought they were overdoing it."[25]

Edward Seaga, the Jamaican Prime Minister and architect of the Grenada invasion had chosen not to attend the Commonwealth meeting. Therefore, it was left to Tom Adams, the Barbados Prime Minister and the leaders of the OECS countries to justify their position. They did so with reasonable success garnering sympathy from the leaders of other small island states and Australia's Prime Minister Bob Hawke.

Ramphal orchestrated it so that the OECS and Barbados leaders were given free rein by the Chair to speak, and he also encouraged the Caribbean leaders who had opposed the invasion not to speak. Thus, Belize and the Bahamas remained silent and the only brief interventions by Chambers (Trinidad and Tobago) and Burnham (Guyana) were to draw attention to a statement being circulated by Chambers of his remarks to his country's parliament in which he described the CARICOM meeting that had been held prior to the invasion. In other words, Ramphal had contrived to ensure that the Caribbean countries did not set upon themselves in the councils of the Commonwealth.

Apart from the Africans, there was no overwhelming mood in the meeting to condemn the Caribbean countries that had participated in the invasion. Lee Kuan Yew, the Prime Minister of Singapore, seemed to sum up the general feeling when he said:

> "Leaders were presented with a paradox: each knew in his heart that the Eastern Caribbean states response was right... it would have been much more convenient if Barbados and Jamaica between them had had the resources to have taken on the Cubans (presumably in Grenada). The matter would then not have been raised at the

meeting, nor would their action have caused great objection in the United Nations, which would have seen it as an example of the Third World resolving its own problems".[26]

In summing up the session, Ramphal made no mention of the differences between the African leaders and the leaders of the Caribbean countries that had participated in the invasion. Instead he focused on what he called "a forward looking approach, particularly one concerned with the recuperation of Grenada and a return to constitutional government." He informed the meeting that he had been "endeavouring to make the Secretariat ready to respond to any requests that might emerge from Grenada, and he had been assisting in the establishment of an Advisory Council, the initial step towards a return to constitutional government."[27]

The Heads of Government went into a retreat on 26 and 27 November in Goa, and it was there that Ramphal circulated three paragraphs that he and his Secretariat team had drafted on Grenada. He ensured that all the Caribbean countries were content with it and he persuaded the leading African countries not to object to it.

This process was so successful that when the entire draft communiqué of the conference came before the Heads of Government who had insisted on seeing it and amending it as they saw fit, the three paragraphs on Grenada were accepted without comment. This acceptance of Ramphal's judgement by leaders who had differed amongst themselves so greatly was a measure of the confidence that they reposed in him. It was at this very meeting that he was elected as Commonwealth Secretary-General for an unprecedented third term.

The section of the Communiqué on Grenada did four important things:
- It agreed that the emphasis should be on reconstruction not recrimination, and affirmed the Commonwealth's readiness to help;
- In welcoming an interim administration, it did so with the expectation that it would function free of external interference, pressure, or the presence of foreign military forces;
- It emphasised that the Commonwealth leaders attached great importance to the early return by Commonwealth Caribbean countries to the spirit of fraternity and co-operation that had

been characteristic of the region; and

- It required the Secretary-General to undertake a study of the special needs of small states consonant with the right to sovereignty and territorial integrity.

An interesting footnote to the Conference and one that calls into question just how upset the British government was with the US invasion of a Commonwealth country was the fact that Margaret Thatcher wrote to Ronald Reagan reporting on the conference. While her letter remains classified and is not yet available, Reagan's response gives indications of what she wrote. Having thanked her for her letter, he said: "Given the predominate (sic) "non aligned" orientation of most Commonwealth member countries, I understand the difficulties you faced". He then went on to say:

"While we are uncomfortable with several passages in the communiqué, I personally appreciate your efforts to moderate and improve the language of the original drafts."

And, specifically on Grenada, he said:

"I was pleased to note the strong and effective response by OECS countries to the hostile challenges of their position on the Grenada matter. You rightly emphasised we should focus our attention on Grenada's future. Your efforts in pointing the communiqué towards an emphasis on "reconstruction", as well as your government's contributions towards economic assistance to Grenada and the rebuilding of the island's police force, are most welcome."[28]

Ramphal subsequently revealed that he had always felt that Thatcher's reaction to the US invasion was more pretence than real, but he decided to use her public statements against the invasion to help promote the withdrawal of US troops from Grenada and to secure British assistance in the rebuilding process.[29]

Immediately after the Commonwealth conference, Ramphal resumed contact with Scoon and the interim administration that had been appointed in December 1983 with Nicholas Braithwaite as its Chairman.

A two-man Commonwealth Secretariat team visited Grenada from 6 to 16 December to explain the Commonwealth position as stated in the communiqué and to explore ways in which the Commonwealth assistance could be mobilised.[30] They met a stonewall on the withdrawal of US troops and discerned the clear impression that "the views of the OECS, Jamaica and Barbados at present dominate the thinking of the interim administration on security. Any change in the security arrangements would therefore require the prior acceptance of these countries."[31]

In truth, the interim administration and the Governor-General were content to keep the US troops in occupation since the presence of the troops consolidated their positions and their authority. What they wanted from the Commonwealth was assistance in reconstruction but if such assistance "is conditional on acceptance of the New Delhi Communiqué, Grenada could get on well without it."[32]

Ramphal knew that this was the situation when he accepted an invitation from the Interim Administration to visit Grenada on 4 January 1984, and he decided to combine it with visits to the key players in the Caribbean – leaders of the OECS, Jamaica and Barbados. He added the Bahamas, Trinidad and Tobago and Guyana, whose governments had opposed the invasion.

Throughout the visits, he stressed the importance of the withdrawal of US troops and their replacement by policemen drawn from the Caribbean. He emphasised the importance of this in the context of the holding of credible general elections.

The OECS leaders that he saw – Bird (Antigua and Barbuda), Charles (Dominica), Compton (St Lucia) – had no problem with the withdrawal of US troops and their replacement by Caribbean policemen. They were pleased that the Bahamas had agreed to provide policemen for the Caribbean contingent and they particularly welcomed Trinidad and Tobago's agreement to contribute. Tom Adams of Barbados was also content to go along with this. All were agreed that Guyana should not participate in the provision of Caribbean troops since its leader Forbes Burnham had been the most hostile and critical of the invasion and of those Caribbean governments that had been part of it. They were all also very keen that the interim administration should hold early elections, or, in the words of Tom Adams he would "pull out Barbados personnel and allow the operation to mash-up".[33]

The most important meeting was with Jamaica's Prime Minister, Edward Seaga, who was clearly in regular contact with the US administration and who was guiding the thinking of the Interim Administration through the Jamaican public servant, Alan Kirton, the Deputy Chairman. Seaga was obviously not in favour of the withdrawal of US troops. He said that "the emphasis should be on building up a major military presence in Grenada as a tangible manifestation of the resolve of governments of the region to defend themselves." It was his view that the US troops "might have to remain for about a year – in any case until after the elections."[34]

Ramphal's view of all this was summarised in his own note at the end of the meeting with Seaga. He wrote:

"SSR and party left Jamaica feeling uneasy about the outcome of the mission... Certainly there was little to encourage belief that Jamaica would be helpful. Rather the contrary. Seaga seems to be directing policy for Grenada... As the mission left Jamaica, it felt it had now heard the definitive reaction: American forces, however small, would remain in Grenada. The Commonwealth should keep out of the law and order situation and limit its role to providing some money to help Grenada... That was the same line that SSR had been given in Washington when he called on the State Department on 20 December, 1983. Both heard from SSR that this was not on."[35]

Ramphal left the region disappointed with the result of his visit to Grenada and Jamaica in particular. He knew then that the Commonwealth could play no role in Grenada at that time. But, at least he had averted a Commonwealth crisis at the Heads of Government Conference and he was successful in getting Caribbean leaders to talk with each other again.

When the Interim Administration, together with the Caribbean governments that had invaded Grenada, announced that US troops would remain in the country, Ramphal issued a terse press release stating that the decision was "a setback to the 'healing process' in relations between Caribbean countries that the Commonwealth sought at New Delhi". He said Commonwealth leaders had looked forward in a spirit of 'reconstruction' to the interim administration in Grenada 'functioning free of external interference, pressure or the presence of foreign military forces'. The Secretariat had tried to help in the phasing out of foreign forces and their replacement by a Commonwealth support unit. And he ended by saying: "the Secretary-General will now report on his efforts to Commonwealth governments generally; but will not propose any further initiatives."

In September 1984, he received a request from the Interim Administration in Grenada to witness general elections set down for 3 December. He duly circulated the request to Commonwealth governments and received negative replies from all who chose to respond. The communication from Kenneth Kaunda, the President of Zambia, summed up the Commonwealth response. In a letter to Ramphal, he said:

"As long as foreign military forces continue to be deployed in Grenada up to the election time and after, Zambia cannot support the presence of a Commonwealth Observer Team, because to support such a suggestion would be contrary to the Commonwealth Summit decision of last year in New Delhi on the matter."[36]

Ramphal informed the Grenada administration of the Commonwealth's position.

Elections were held while US troops were in occupation and with "state trials" in process in relation to the events of October 1983. These factors would have influenced both the decisions of persons to form themselves into parties to contest the elections and the participation by the electorate in the vote.

Reflecting on his feelings at the time Ramphal continues to believe that the Caribbean let itself down through the majority who sided with an American invasion of their region – and those among them who participated actively in engineering it. The vote in the UN General Assembly, he believes, undid credits that the Caribbean had worked hard to build up in the years since Jamaica's and Trinidad and Tobago's independence in 1962. It was specially hard for him as a Caribbean man; but he says he takes comfort in the robustness with which the Commonwealth stood on the side of internationalism.[37]

But the Grenada episode was not all a dark spot for the Caribbean and the Commonwealth. Aware that small countries would continue to be susceptible to the internal conditions that caused the coup d'état in

Grenada in 1979 and again in 1983, and to the risk of invasion by larger powers intent upon procuring their own interests, Ramphal had ensured that he had received a mandate from the New Delhi Commonwealth Summit for a study of the special needs of small states, including their security needs.

In 1984, he appointed a distinguished group drawn from small and large states of the Commonwealth to produce the study. They did so in August 1985. It was entitled, "Vulnerability: Small States in the Global Society." It became a seminal document on the problems of small states, informing the work not only of the Commonwealth, but also the United Nations, the World Bank and the International Monetary Fund.

The US-led invasion of Grenada with the connivance of some Caribbean countries – many of whom were motivated by genuine fear – is not a part of the Caribbean's proudest heritage. But, that some Caribbean countries stood against it, and that the Commonwealth, over whose Secretariat a Caribbean man presided at the time, became a flag bearer for the cause of ending the invasion and returning Grenada to democratic government, is all on the credit side. One of its legacies, moreover, was the place that Ramphal engineered for "small states" on the international agenda, and on that agenda item all the Caribbean is united.

1   The OECS was formed in 1981 and consisted of: Antigua and Barbuda, Dominica, Grenada, St Kitts-Nevis, St Lucia, St Vincent and the Grenadines and Montserrat

2   Telex message 27678 to Comsec from St Lucia Foreign Ministry on behalf of the OECS Secretariat addressed to Secretary-General, Commonwealth Secretariat on 25 October 1983.

3   Ramphal, S.S., Statement by Commonwealth Secretary-General, issued on 25 October 1983, Commonwealth Secretariat, London

4   Interview with Ramphal by the author, January 2008

5   Observations by the Secretary of State for Foreign and Commonwealth Affairs, in Second Report from the Foreign Affairs Committee Session 1983-1984 on Grenada; HMSO, London, June 1984.

6   "Grenada: A Preliminary Report", released by the Department of State and the Department of Defense", Washington, D.C., 16 December 1983, p.8.

7   Ronald Reagan, US President, Op. Cit,. 10 March 1983 at the Washington Hilton, see: www.thegrenadarevolutiononline.com/reaganspeech031083.html

8   Communiqué issued at the conclusion of the Third Conference of the Heads of Government of the Caribbean Community, 16-18 November 1982, Ocho Rios, Jamaica. See: www.caricom.org/jsp/communications/communiques/3hgc_1982_communique.jsp

9   See: George Chambers, Prime Minister of Trinidad and Tobago, Speech before Parliament of Trinidad and Tobago, on the Grenada issue, 26 October 1983,

10   Letter dated 24 October 1983 from US President Ronald Reagan to British Prime Minister Margaret Thatcher. See: www.margaretthatcher.org/archive/displaydocument.asp?docid=109428

11   Second letter dated 24 October 1983 from Reagan to Thatcher. See: www.margaretthatcher.org/archive/displaydocument.asp?docid=109429

12   See: www.margaretthatcher.org/commentary/displaydocument.asp?docid= 109427

13   www.margaretthatcher.org/archive/displaydocument.asp?docid=109426

14   Interview with Sonny Ramphal, Commonwealth Secretary-General, on the BBC's "Today" programme on 26 October 1983

15   Ibid

16   Op.Cit., Note 2

17   Op. Cit., Note 3.

18   Op. Cit., Note 6, p.2

19   Note by Shridath Ramphal of his conversation with Sir Paul Scoon on Friday 28 October at 3pm (London time) from the Ramphal papers held at the Cave Hill Campus of the University of the West Indies, Barbados.

20   Note by Shridath Ramphal of his conversation with Alister McIntyre on 28 October 1983 from the Ramphal papers held at the Cave Hill Campus of the University of the West Indies, Barbados.

21   Note by Shridath Ramphal of his conversation with Sir Paul Scoon on Saturday 29 October at 2pm (London time) from the Ramphal papers held at the Cave Hill Campus of the University of the West Indies, Barbados.

22   Minutes of Sessions and Memoranda, Commonwealth Heads of Government Meeting, New Delhi, 23-29 November 1983. p.4.

23   Ibid., pp 61-62.

24   Ibid., p.63.

25   Ibid., p.82.

26   Ibid., p.83

27   Ibid., p.91.

28   See: www.margaretthatcher.org/archive/displaydocument.asp?docid=109339

29   Interview with Ramphal by the author in Barbados, January 2008

30   The team consisted of David Anderson and Karl Dundas.

31   Report on their mission to Grenada by David Anderson and Karl Dundas in the Ramphal papers held at the Cave Hill Campus, University of the West Indies, Barbados.

32   This was contained in a Note written by David Anderson on 5 January 1984 of a discussion with Dr (Patrick) Emmanuel (member of the Interim administration) in Grenada on 13 December 1983 at 8pm. The note is in the Ramphal papers held at the Cave Hill Campus, University of the West Indies, Barbados.

33 Note of meetings between Ramphal and Caribbean Heads of Government, the Grenada Interim Administration and the Governor-General between 1st and 9th January 1984, in the Ramphal papers held at the Cave Hill Campus, University of the West Indies, Barbados.

34 Note of meeting between Ramphal and Seaga on 9th January 1984, in the Ramphal papers held at the Cave Hill Campus, University of the West Indies, Barbados.

35 Ibid., p. 5

36 Op. Cit., letter dated 27 November 1984 in the Ramphal papers held at the Cave Hill Campus, University of the West Indies, Barbados.

37 Interview with Ramphal by the author, January 2008

Statesman of the West Indies

Anthony Payne

— ∞ —

Sonny Ramphal is of course not only a Commonwealth statesman; he was a statesman of the West Indies long before he was drawn towards Marlborough House and he actively resumed that role as soon as he stood down from his position as Commonwealth Secretary-General. Indeed, like so many others who left different parts of the Caribbean and travelled for various reasons to the United Kingdom, Ramphal only fully came to acknowledge that he was a West Indian during the first period of time that he spent in London. He began his legal training at King's College in 1947 and was called to the bar from Gray's Inn in 1951. He began work as a pupil in chambers in London, continued studying for a Master's degree in law and helped out part-time in the legal section of the Colonial Office as a further means of supporting himself.

At some point in the early 1950s the young Ramphal, still only in his early twenties, attended a lecture given at the London School of Economics by Norman Washington (N.W.) Manley. As he reported many years later in his Norman Manley Memorial Lecture, he immediately fell under Manley's 'spell'. "The preparatory work on West Indian federation was gathering momentum," Ramphal recalled, and "Manley shared with us – some of the generation that would play a part in its unfolding – his vision of the future West Indian nation." He went on, tellingly: "It is a vision I have never lost – or lost faith in."[1]

In the same lecture Ramphal also talked about the collapse of the West Indies Federation (of which more shortly) and, in a highly revealing turn of phrase, noted that the issue that had necessarily to preoccupy

— ∞ —

Professor Anthony Payne is Professor of Politics at Sheffield University and author of several books on the modern Caribbean.

him thereafter was "the prospects for the Caribbean – no longer the West Indies."[2] That was, and remains, the reality as far as the political structure of the region is concerned. But, in deference to and respect for Ramphal's vision of what the Caribbean needs to become, I have preferred to use the title "Statesman of the West Indies," rather than "Statesman of the Caribbean."

The essay will unfold in three parts, of which two, the first and third, will be the longer. Part 1 will examine Ramphal's record as a regional statesman in the period from 1953 to 1975 when he left the Caribbean to become Commonwealth Secretary-General. Part 2 (much more briefly) will review economic and political developments in the Caribbean whilst Ramphal was active on the Commonwealth front. Part 3 will then pick up his re-involvement in Caribbean affairs and carry the story through from 1990 to the present. A short conclusion will then attempt to sum up Ramphal's contribution to the modern history of the West Indies.

RAMPHAL IN THE CARIBBEAN 1953 – 75

Ramphal returned from London to his native British Guiana (as it then still was) in 1953 and took up a position as crown counsel in the Attorney-General's office in Georgetown. This was an extraordinarily turbulent time in the colony's politics. The first serious elections to be held under universal suffrage took place in April of that year and resulted in a sweeping victory for the People's Progressive Party (PPP), a radical nationalist movement, jointly led by Forbes Burnham and Cheddi Jagan, that for a time drew on the support of both the African and East Indian elements of the country's population.

However, after just a few months, the British governor dismissed the PPP from office, suspended the colony's constitution on the grounds that the country was being threatened with communist subversion and, supported by British troops and officials, took over responsibility for government himself. The PPP thereafter split into racial factions, led separately by Burnham and Jagan, and nationalist politics in British Guiana never again fully regained its equilibrium. Ramphal has not said much in public about this period, but it is obvious that he was uncomfortable with Jagan's openly Marxist brand of progressive politics. He focused his attention on issues of constitutional law and began to think about the nature and structure of a constitution for an independent West Indian state. His interest in such issues was noticed and in 1958 he left the country of his birth to move to Port of Spain in Trinidad to join the new Federal Government of the West Indies as legal draftsman. It proved to be but a short posting: within approximately a year he was "recalled" to Georgetown as a consequence of a crisis in the Attorney-General's office there and promoted to the high office of Solicitor-General of British Guiana.

Yet it seems as if Ramphal was destined to be drawn back towards the Federation, because in early 1961 he was again persuaded to return to Port of Spain to work in the newly created post of Assistant Attorney-General. In this position he was centrally involved in the drafting of the planned independence constitution of the Federation, attending and playing a part in the so-called London conference that set the date for the independence of the West Indies as 31 May 1962. Ramphal has described the mood of that meeting as cheerless, given the travails already being experienced by the Federation and the popular support for independent statehood that was building dangerously in Jamaica, and has noted that, even as delegates ended the meeting, "we were conscious that it was an independence that might never dawn."[3]

So it proved: following the defeat of Norman Manley and the pro-Federation cause in a referendum in Jamaica in September 1961 and the subsequent decision of Trinidad and Tobago also to pursue a national route to independence, the Federation was dissolved, in an awful irony, on the very day that had earlier been set as the moment of birth of an independent West Indian state. Like so many educated and politically aware West Indians of his generation Ramphal experienced the collapse of the Federation as an "acute disappointment," although he was later honest enough to admit that his emotions at the time also bordered on "petulance."[4] His political dream had been shattered, and maybe too what he thought of as his deserved inheritance as a politically conscious West Indian.

Indeed, it would not be too much to say that Ramphal has been haunted ever since by the failure of the Federation. More than once in speeches and other public occasions he has reflected sadly upon what might have been, if the referendum vote in Jamaica had not sawn off the Federal experiment in the Caribbean before it had properly begun.
    "Might Grantley Adams [the Barbadian Prime Minister of the

Federation between 1958 and 1962] not have moved over soon after Independence and made way for Norman Manley as Federal Prime Minister – a Manley strengthened and reassured by the 'Yes' vote at home? And with Manley committed now to making the Federal Government effective, would not the gap between himself and Eric Williams [the Premier of Trinidad and Tobago at the time of the Federation] that had opened up in the last stages of the federal negotiations, would not that gap have narrowed? Would they not have come together with shared incentive and commitment to a strong Federal Government founded on the 'economics of nationhood'? And with the Federation barely two years old, would not Guyana, with its Interim Government dissolved and elections held in 1964 – would not Guyana have quickly joined the Federation, changing the political arithmetic so that thereafter it would not always be 1 from 10 but 1 from 11: the secession of any one member – however large – leaving not nought, but one, a federal unit? And would not Belize and the Bahamas, before the 60s were out, have confirmed the region's federal destiny".[5]

His speculations are fascinating and, although it is more than possible to find arguments with which to challenge such an optimistic prognosis, it is not so easy to dismiss completely the overall thrust of his golden scenario. At the very least, as he himself put it in the speech in 1985 in which he allowed himself to muse so interestingly about alternative regional histories that might have been, "options for the Caribbean would now be rather different."

Instead, Ramphal left Port of Spain on 30 August 1962 – a date that he has described, pointedly, as the day after Jamaica's independence and the day before Trinidad's – to take up a one-year Guggenheim Fellowship at Harvard Law School. He then returned to the Caribbean, taking up residence in Jamaica, the country that had done most to wreck the Federation, and practising law in Kingston in the chambers of Harvey Da Costa, a friend and former colleague who had been his superior as Federal Attorney-General. This was a not unimportant moment in the making of Ramphal's politics, because he has subsequently stated that he "received at the hands of Jamaicans ... an acceptance and a friendship of a very special quality" that "did much to sustain my faith in the reality of a West Indian identity during those years of despair in the early 1960s."[6]

At this point in his life he might perhaps have settled for a distinguished and lucrative career at the bar. But, in British Guiana in the meantime, politics had moved on. Jagan continued to lead the PPP, whereas Burnham had formed a new political party called the People's National Congress (PNC). Each came to rely more and more on a core of ethnic support, with East Indians increasingly identifying with the PPP and the Afro-Guyanese with the PNC. A small party called the United Force (UF) represented business. A new constitution had also been devised in the Colonial Office in London as the means by which to move the colony to independence: it was based on proportional representation and had been explicitly designed by the United Kingdom, in conjunction with its Cold War ally, the United States, to contain the electoral prospects of the Marxist-inclined PPP. The scheme worked entirely according to plan.

Following elections held in December 1964, Forbes Burnham emerged as the leader of a PNC-UF coalition government. By comparison with Jagan at least, he was deemed to be the acceptable face of nationalism in British Guiana and he was given permission to lead British Guiana to independence (as Guyana) in 1966. Burnham had not forgotten Ramphal and he called him in Kingston and implored him to return home, to become Attorney-General in his government, and to begin the task of drafting Guyana's independence constitution. The "challenge of shaping a new Guyana" was "an invitation, an offer if you will," that Ramphal could not refuse and he returned to politics and to Georgetown in early 1965.[7]

Ramphal now had a political base from which to operate, not only in Guyana but also in the wider politics of the Commonwealth Caribbean. He worked in the various governments of Forbes Burnham for just over ten years, becoming Minister of State for External Affairs as well as Attorney-General in 1967 and then in 1972 being appointed to head a renamed Ministry of Foreign Affairs. A year later he also took on the portfolio of Minister of Justice. He thus played a central role in equipping the country with a foreign service and in charting Guyana's foreign policy in these early days of its independent history.

He had to think harder than most people about what it meant for a new state to make its way on the international scene and he offered his reflections on these issues in a statement made to a seminar at the

University of the West Indies in Trinidad in 1967. He argued that a country's foreign policy could not be simply, and naively, selected like a national flag or anthem. It could "only be hammered out on the anvil of experience and amid the heat and dust of the busy workshop of international affairs." But, he went on,

"What we can insist upon, is the right to devise a foreign policy on the basis of experience and one that is tailored to our needs, rather than be expected, through an almost axiomatic identification with the power struggles of greater nations, to adopt one fully fashioned to the requirements of causes not our own. It is ... this demand for acknowledgement of the right of self-determination in the area of foreign affairs which lies at the heart of the concept of neutralism or non-alignment that has been the central theme of the foreign policy of so many of the new States".[8]

Under Ramphal's stewardship non-alignment did indeed become the organising theme of Guyana's early foreign policy. Inheriting from the outset a longstanding claim by Venezuela to an enormous portion of its territory, Guyana needed to make friends quickly. It could just have looked for support in London and Washington and cut its diplomatic cloth accordingly. It chose to move in another direction, taking initial advantage of the country's location on the South American mainland to open up to several of its continental neighbours and then to move on from those openings to play a wider role within the Commonwealth, the Group of 77 (or "developing") countries at the United Nations and the Non-Aligned Movement (NAM) itself. Burnham possessed the loudest and most strident voice in proclaiming these affiliations, but Ramphal was often the craftsman that had engineered the relationships in the first place.

However, even in the midst of initiating these diverse and demanding new forms of diplomacy, Guyana did not lose sight of its West Indian identity. Indeed, it took the lead in this period in seeking to rebuild some basis for West Indian unity, initially in December 1965 by taking steps to sign an agreement to establish a putative Caribbean Free Trade Association (CARIFTA) between itself, Barbados and Antigua. Ramphal has explained this activist approach by noting that, since Guyana had not taken part in the Federation experiment, its emissaries were able to bring to a somewhat chastened Caribbean "a refreshing enthusiasm for co-operation and, no less important, to be received in all quarters without antagonism and suspicion bred of past conflicts'.[9] Ramphal himself had come more realistically to recognise that, as he later put it, 'the natural state of our Caribbean is fragmentation'[10] and that constant effort was needed to build and then preserve workable mechanisms of integration.

The widening of CARIFTA to embrace the whole of the Commonwealth Caribbean in 1968 and its subsequent growth into the Caribbean Community and Common Market (CARICOM) in 1973 was thus "a triumph of practicality over inclination,"[11] not an expression of the heroic road to regionalism, but nevertheless a necessary, if always tortuous and often awkward, process which independent Commonwealth Caribbean states had to be coaxed to pursue. As the various historical accounts show, Ramphal was a crucial player during the "decade of decision"[12] in which the foundations of Caribbean integration were re-laid. His hand can be found upon many of the diplomatic compromises which ensured CARICOM's creation and development, not least the drafting of the crucial Georgetown Accord of April 1973 which prevented a rift emerging between the smaller "less developed" and the larger "more developed" countries of the region.

For Ramphal, this was indeed a vintage period.[13] There was encouraging evidence that on a number of issues the Commonwealth Caribbean region was managing to rise above considerations of short-term national interest and he was totally absorbed in making that happen. Looking back over these years he said on one occasion:

"I remember well how convinced an advocate I became of the concept of the "Regional Carrier;" how hard we worked to find a common position in the then still early Law of the Sea discussions. I remember with particular satisfaction the leadership the Caribbean gave throughout the negotiations that led to the first Lomé Convention when, because the region had first united itself, it was able to be a unifying influence between Francophone and English-speaking African countries and then to mould the ACP [African, Caribbean and Pacific countries] into an effective negotiating group. The essence of that effort was hard work, patient, persevering preparation in the Caribbean, with the region's technicians responding to the challenge of negotiations with the European Community".[14]

This last achievement was very much Ramphal's triumph. It was he more than any other person who was responsible for the creation of the ACP grouping. He used a meeting of the foreign ministers of the Non-Aligned Movement that took place in Georgetown in August 1972 to convene informal talks amongst the Commonwealth members present (some of them literally on the lawns of the Prime Minister's residence during a reception[15]) and propose the adoption of joint positions as far as possible in forthcoming association talks with the European Economic Community. Thereafter he took a leading role in the negotiations in several key areas and, by common consent, conducted affairs with both skill and firmness throughout. The outcome was a set of terms that largely lived up to his stated ambition to deliver 'just, enlightened and effective arrangements'[16] in future relations between the 'developed' EEC countries and the 'developing' ACP countries.

Ramphal had also invited to that NAM meeting in Georgetown in 1972 the foreign minister of Cuba, Raul Roa. This was the country's first appearance at an international gathering (apart from the United Nations itself) in the western hemisphere since the revolution. Cuba wanted to conclude a formal diplomatic agreement with Guyana and the Guyanese government was more than willing to do so. However, it urged deferment of such a decision until other CARICOM partners, namely, Barbados, Jamaica and Trinidad and Tobago, could also be brought on board.

It was therefore something of a diplomatic coup when in October 1972 all the four leading independent Commonwealth Caribbean countries defied the US State Department and established formal diplomatic relations with the Republic of Cuba. Ramphal played a key part in the diplomacy surrounding this announcement and the whole move very much appealed to him. As far as he was concerned, it was "an act rooted not in ideology but in practical regional considerations and the refusal of Caribbean countries to be pawns in a super-power game."[17]

In a passionate and confident last address to the CARICOM heads of government before leaving the Caribbean in 1975 to take up his new post as Commonwealth Secretary-General, Ramphal explicitly urged his colleagues to "care for" CARICOM. It was an unusual choice of phrase that expressed aptly the emotional commitment invested by him in what to others might appear as merely a set of functional economic and political arrangements.

For Ramphal's argument was that CARICOM, for all of its shortcomings and failures to act, which he knew better than most, was nevertheless the custodian of the idea of West Indian nationhood. It was, for better or worse, the body that had to hold the region together until the moment was right to move on from economic to political integration. That did not mean that he shied away completely from talking about his continuing belief in the case for Caribbean political integration. For example, he supported the Grenada Declaration of July 1971 in which the heads of government of six Commonwealth Caribbean states (Dominica, Guyana, St Lucia, Grenada, St Kitts-Nevis-Anguilla and St Vincent) announced their intention to establish a new state out of their combined territories.

Speaking in November of that year, by which time opposition and backsliding was already apparent, he urged the leaders "to stop the chat and begin the work."[18] However, nothing emerged from this or other such initiatives in the early 1970s and that undoubtedly raised the question in Ramphal's mind as to whether the real political choice facing the region was either "to evoke appropriate forms of political unity or face the erosion of the institutions of mutual assistance we have so far established."[19] In the final analysis, his view was that CARICOM would not be properly cared for (to use his phrase) until it had grown incrementally into some form – although not necessarily federal – of political union.

RAMPHAL AND THE CARIBBEAN 1975 – 90

Ramphal then spent the next 15 years of his career working in London as the Commonwealth Secretary-General. It was obviously an honour for the Caribbean as a region that he was appointed to such a position – the first person from a poor, non-white Commonwealth country to be so elevated. But the protocol of the position meant that he could only speak out when Commonwealth, rather than specifically Caribbean, interests were at stake. He was also heavily preoccupied, given the context of the times, with the South Africa question. The only real occasion when a Caribbean crisis crossed his desk occurred in October 1983 when United States troops invaded Grenada, a member country of the Commonwealth, in circumstances that raised doubts as to whether the island's Governor-General, who was the representative of the Queen as head of the Commonwealth, had, or had not, invited them to do so.

The Queen's own reported dismay at the US action enabled Ramphal to be more outspoken about the invasion than perhaps would otherwise have been the case. More importantly, though, the Commonwealth's response to Grenada was to widen the whole issue, to highlight the great vulnerability of small island states in general to security threats, economic instability and environmental degradation. It initiated a programme of research and policy advice designed to help its constituent small member countries that has run to the present day and has helped such states, including those in the Commonwealth Caribbean, to ward off some of the constraints imposed by limitations of size.

The fact that Grenada had been invaded by the USA in the cause of bringing to an end a communist revolution did, however, show how much the political temperature of the region had changed, even in the first few years that Ramphal was away. CARICOM plans to deepen the level of regional economic integration were largely set aside in the face of global economic difficulties in the second half of the 1970s. These played themselves out in the region in the form of a growing "ideological pluralism" (as it was dubbed) whereby some governments moved to the left and others to the right. President Reagan's assumption of office in the USA added further tensions, locating regional politics within a framework of renewed Cold War thinking.

Clumsy attempts were made to expel revolutionary Grenada from CARICOM on the grounds that its political system was no longer a parliamentary democracy and then the region's leaders fell into acrimonious argument about the legitimacy of the invasion of the island itself. In short, the mood had changed, and changed quickly, from the heady optimism of those informal conversations in Georgetown in 1972 when the ACP was being conceived and openings to Cuba planned. Ramphal noticed all of this, of course, and spoke about it thoughtfully in a lecture he gave at the University of Warwick in 1985 to mark the opening of its new Centre for Caribbean Studies.

> "In a curious way, that early manifestation of regional unity in areas where it mattered most was achieved in an environment within the region that was tolerant of pluralism; tolerant of shades of difference

– ideological and otherwise – among the countries of the region. Ironically, that unity fell away when the environment of the region became unpropitious to pluralism. It might seem paradoxical, but it is really intelligible, that when a group becomes intolerant of the differences within itself, it moves not to homogeneity but to fragmentation – the very environment of intolerance encouraging fissiparous trends. The differences tolerated before, and here and there overcome in the interests of joint positions, become now ever-deeper diversions. And that in large measure has been the fate of the Caribbean over something like the last decade".[20]

The confidence, ebullience and sheer optimism that had marked all of Ramphal's many other speeches and writings about the Caribbean were notably missing, replaced instead by a weariness and deeper sadness that the region's options were now much more limited than they had been 20 years earlier.

The other dimension to this sense of diminished possibilities was the shift that had also taken place on the wider world stage, which again Ramphal was well placed to observe from his vantage point in Marlborough House. In a nutshell, this is to say that the broad ideological consensus around international social democracy that had give birth to the UN and to the Bretton Woods institutions in the years after 1945 was being replaced by a new, harsher neoliberalism, espoused by leaders like Reagan in the USA and Mrs Thatcher in the UK, that saw the rigours of the market as the solution to most problems and rejected accordingly all belief in the existence of something that might truly be called a global neighbourhood.

The key symbolic moment came in October 1981 when Reagan turned his back upon all the demands that were being made by poorer countries for a New International Economic Order at a major summit meeting in Cancún in Mexico. The concept of the Third World as an international actor effectively died at that conference and the world order henceforth became a much more difficult place for political leaders like Ramphal to operate within.

RAMPHAL IN THE CARIBBEAN 1990 – PRESENT

Shortly before coming to the end of his period of service with the Commonwealth Ramphal was asked to return to the Caribbean to plead one more time for a major advance in CARICOM. He was invited by the heads of government to lead an independent West Indian Commission, composed of prominent regional figures from the bureaucracy, business, labour, the church and education and charged with the task of plotting a course for the region post-1992, the year of the 500th anniversary of Columbus's 'discovery' of the Caribbean. The task was made for Ramphal: it called upon all of his energy, diplomatic skill and powers of advocacy. As indicated, the situation facing the Commonwealth Caribbean in 1989 when the Commission was appointed was very different from the mood of freshness and hope that had prevailed in the early 1970s just before he left for London. In marked contrast to the heady euphoria generated by the signing of Lomé, what now stared the region was the prospect of marginalisation as new centres of power emerged in a global political economy increasingly characterised by the ethics of competitiveness and reciprocity, not those of obligation and preference. Indeed, it was the very task of how to avoid marginalisation that was handed to the West Indian Commission by a worried gathering of heads of government.

Ramphal ran the Commission with great style. It was inevitably compared with the enquiry undertaken by Lord Moyne on behalf of the British government after the riots and disturbances that ran through the English-speaking Caribbean in the 1930s and it is true that the scale of the exercise was as grand. What the comparison misses, however, is the extent of the democratic impulse that underpinned the Commission's work. As its members travelled throughout the region and in the major locations of the West Indian diaspora in the UK, the USA and Canada, holding meetings wherever they went with local elites but also with members of the ordinary public, they encountered an extraordinary and patently moving outpouring of West Indian sentiment.

The peoples of the Caribbean wanted better for their region and said so in their own distinctive and colourful way. In his preface to the commission's final report Ramphal himself spoke of some of his particular recollections – a young Amerindian woman speaking out publicly in Georgetown's City Hall, a meeting in a dimly lit school hall in a fishing village in St Vincent, sixth-formers in Port of Spain expressing their anxieties about the future, "grounding" with some Rastafarians in Barbados, an evening talking with Fidel Castro in Cuba and so on.[21] All in all, the commission had the potential to be one of the defining post-Federation moments of the modern Caribbean.

Its proposals were appropriately bold, as the two speeches given by Ramphal at the time of his presentation of the commission's interim and final reports amply demonstrate.[22] By his own admission, "the central decision" that the Caribbean heads of government were urged to take was the establishment of a Caribbean Commission, composed initially of three persons with high-level public and political experience in the region and designed explicitly to oversee the simultaneous deepening and widening of the regional integration movement.[23] It is not too much to say that the whole strategy of development for CARICOM outlined in the final report, which was provocatively entitled *Time for Action*, depended on this proposal, for the new Commission was seen as the motor that could drive the organisation forward that it had so singularly lacked hitherto.

Significantly, Ramphal's team did not choose to embrace a return to federalism or any other form of political union. It was believed that "this would be going too far, attempting too much, out-stripping our regional capacities at this time."[24] The commission idea was presented accordingly as a modest initiative, at least by comparison. For all that, it was rejected by the heads of government. There were several reasons, but one was undoubtedly their reluctance to have retired ex-leaders (including Ramphal himself) interfering, as they plainly saw it, in national sovereign affairs. It did not matter that Ramphal had said quite unequivocally on behalf of himself and the other authors of the report that "we envisage no roles for ourselves in that new machinery."[25]

From the nation-building perspective, the unfortunate fact was that the newer leaders holding office in the Commonwealth Caribbean in the 1990s felt the force of West Indian nationalism with markedly less emotion than the leading figures of the previous generation. As a result, although several of the detailed recommendations of the report were accepted and new bodies were subsequently instituted, such as the Association of Caribbean States, composed of all the member-states of the Caribbean Basin, the opportunity that the West Indian Commission offered – which was to lift CARICOM's whole operation to a new level of seriousness concomitant with the gravity of the challenges facing the region – was not grasped.

Ramphal must have felt a huge sense of disappointment, even if it not quite as acute as that he had experienced in 1962 at the time of the demise of the Federation. He was, after all, a good deal older and more familiar with the ways of island politics in the Caribbean, better able in his mid-sixties perhaps to see and play the longer game. Even so, he can hardly have expected at this point to play another major innings in Commonwealth Caribbean affairs. Yet this is what ensued.

In 1997 the CARICOM heads decided to set up a new institution – the Caribbean Regional Negotiating Machinery (RNM) – to handle the various complicated and interlinked trade negotiations (with the European Union post-Lomé, with the rest of the Americas and with the rest of the world in respect of a planned new trade round) that were then converging upon the Caribbean. Who did they eventually ask to head this new body? The answer is of course Ramphal. He seized the opportunity to impose his own persona on the design of the RNM, insisting on several significant changes in the original thinking, such as the upgrading of the chief negotiator from ambassadorial to ministerial rank and the establishment of the RNM's operational base in London, where he resided, rather than in Barbados as initially intended. He also laid out the RNM's mandate in a series of classic Ramphal propositions.

He argued, first, that the RNM concept did not prevent Caribbean countries taking up their places at the negotiating table; second, that they must, however, all "sing from the same hymn sheet[26];" third, that the objective was not to choose between Europe and the Americas but rather to keep open as many "windows to the world" as possible[27]; and, fourth, that solidarity beyond the region, both within the old ACP grouping and amongst small and vulnerable countries more generally, was vital to the strengthening of the Caribbean negotiating position. Beyond these points, he also signalled that he had adjusted to the times and had come to recognise reciprocity as an imperative. In his words, "we may win time to adjust to that change; but we have to be prepared in our minds for a world in which our markets will be open increasingly to competition and not only at the level of goods but also of investment and services."[28]

This is not the place to review in full the RNM's work. It was unquestionably given a most difficult brief and it is not surprising that it was at times fully stretched to cope. Nor, given the new neoliberal consensus, was there ever remotely the possibility that Ramphal could engineer another Lomé-type diplomatic triumph. That was simply an impossibility. Ramphal eventually stood down as the Caribbean's chief negotiator after the conclusion of the World Trade Organization Ministerial Conference held in Doha in November 2001. By then he was aged 73 and long overdue a deserved retirement. This has, however, not quite yet come about.

Since relinquishing his RNM position, Ramphal has been called upon further: to act as the Facilitator for Belize in talks with a Facilitator for Guatemala conducted under the auspices of the Organisation of American States in September 2002 in an attempt to find a solution to the long-running Belize-Guatemala territorial dispute; to chair between July 2003 and February 2005 a CARICOM "prime ministerial expert group on governance" that again called for the establishment of a Caribbean Commission broadly along the lines previously proposed by the West Indian Commission; and to lead Guyana's team over the period 2004-7 in successfully presenting its case to an arbitration tribunal established under the terms of the UN Law of the Sea Convention in relation to that country's territorial dispute with Suriname.

There may indeed be other tasks and duties still to come. It would be silly to presume otherwise. Certainly, nobody involved with or interested in the Caribbean can doubt but that Ramphal has fully lived up to the personal inscription that the late Dr Eric Williams wrote in the copy of his book *From Columbus to Castro* that he gave to Ramphal. It said simply: 'We are both labourers in the vineyard'.[29]

CONCLUSION

What, finally, does this extraordinary record of West Indian statesmanship add up to by way of achievement? Ramphal has always been an honest and realistic man and his own answer to that question might well be that his political life in the Caribbean has been associated as much with failure as success. After all, the West Indies Federation, his political dream, was dissolved when he was only 33 years old; it has not been reinstated since and it is extremely unlikely that it ever will be. He and others came up with the notion of a Caribbean Commission as something of a half-way house between economic and political integration in the Commonwealth Caribbean. It too has not come into being as yet, but the idea is still on the table before regional heads of government, thanks very much to Ramphal's continuing efforts, and that in itself will be gratifying to him.

It should also be said, moreover, that CARICOM itself is an achievement not to be dismissed. It has disappointed, to be sure, always seeming to move too slowly and to adopt proposals when it is too late for them to have the impact that was initially expected. But it has served to keep the regional idea alive, which was the rationale for CARICOM that Ramphal and others saw so clearly back in that decade of decision from 1965 to 1975. As we have seen again and again, however, Ramphal has also always taken a deeply emotional stance towards issues of West Indian unity. On the occasion on the conferment upon him of the Honorary Degree of Doctor of Laws by the University of the West Indies (which he also served from 1989 to 2003 as Chancellor, in itself another substantial contribution to public service) he opened his address with the following credo:

> "In that sense of being that derives from within, is assured and unchanging, I have been a West Indian from the first moments of my rational awakening. The land of my birth, my country that I was privileged to help to bring to sovereign statehood, commands my devotion and my loyalty; but, in a further dimension of belonging, the West Indies is, also, my native land".[30]

He then added, poignantly: "I trust that I am not in this regard a member of a vanishing tribe." That remark was made as long ago as January 1978 and reads now as a highly insightful observation on changing times. For Ramphal is a representative of a breed of West Indian that is not being produced any more.

Further steps forward in the making of West Indian unity will not derive their essential impetus from sentiments such as these, for they are weaker than they were. But such advances may still yet emerge out of necessity and desperation, out of an urgent need to find a workable niche in a globalising world order. In these circumstances, should they ever occur, it will have been vital that the basic edifice of contemporary regional unity, the CARICOM system, was put in place and thereafter preserved and nurtured. The fact that this took place is in large part a consequence of Sonny Ramphal's tireless endeavour and creative statesmanship over a period of many years.

— ∞ —

1   S Ramphal, 'No island is an island', in D Dabydeen & J Gilmore (eds), *No Island is an Island: Selected Speeches of Sir Shridath Ramphal* (London and Oxford: Warwick University Caribbean Studies for Macmillan Education, 2000), p. 14.

2   Ibid., p. 15.

3   S Ramphal, *West Indian Nationhood: Myth, Mirage or Mandate?*, opening address in a series on 'Caribbean Perspectives', Public Library, Port of Spain, 26 May 1971 (Georgetown: Ministry of External Affairs, 1971), p.7.

4   Ramphal, 'No island is an island', p. 15.

5   S Ramphal, *'The Lure of Realpolitik'*, speech delivered in the Distinguished Lecturer Series sponsored by the Institute of International Relations of the University of the West Indies, mimeo, 13 May 1985.

6   S Ramphal, *To Care for CARICOM: The Need for an Ethos of Community*, speech delivered at a dinner held in Ramphal's honour by the CARICOM Council of Ministers, Montego Bay, 5 July 1975, p. 3.

7   Ibid.

8   S Ramphal, *Building the Foundations*, the text of a lecture given at the Carnegic seminar on Diplomacy at the Institute of International Affairs, University of the West Indies, St Augustine, Trinidad, June (Georgetown: Government Printery, 1967), p. 5.

9   S Ramphal, *The Prospect for Community in the Caribbean*, an address delivered at the Royal Commonwealth Society, London, 22 January 1973 (Georgetown: Ministry of Foreign Affairs, 1973), p. 4.

10 Ramphal, *To Care for CARICOM*, p. 7.

11 S Ramphal, *Caribbean Alternatives*, an address to mark the opening of the Centre for Caribbean Studies, University of Warwick, 9 May 1985 (Warwick: Centre for Caribbean Studies, 1985), p. 8.

12 S Ramphal, *Decade of Decision: The Caribbean in the 70s*, an address delivered to the National Press Club of Trinidad and Tobago, 20 March 1970 (Georgetown: Ministry of External Affairs), p. 8.

13 Ramphal, Caribbean Alternatives, p. 9.

14 Ibid., pp. 8-9.

15 S Ramphal, *'Remembering to Score'*, a retrospective for the souvenir issue of Perspective, mimeo, no date.

16 S Ramphal, *Just, Enlightened and Effective Arrangements: New Approach to Relations with the European Economic Community*, statement delivered at the Opening Conference on Relations between the EEC and the ACP on Behalf of the Delegation of Caribbean Countries, Brussels, 26 July 1973 (Georgetown: Ministry of Foreign Affairs, 1973).

17 Ramphal, *Caribbean Alternatives*, p. 9.

18 S Ramphal, *Dialogue of Unity: A Search for West Indian Identity*, an address delivered at the Caribbean Ecumenical Consultation for Development, Chaguaramas, 16 November 1971 (Georgetown: Ministry of External Affairs, 1971), p. 22.

19 Ibid., p.15.

20 Ramphal, *Caribbean Alternatives*, p. 11.

21   S Ramphal, 'Chairman's Preface', in West Indian Commission, *Time for Action: Report of the West Indian Commission* (Black Rock, Barbados: West Indian Commission, 1992), pp. xxiii-xxiv.

22   S Ramphal, 'To be a Canoe', presentation to the 12th Conference of Heads of Government of the Caribbean Community, Basseterre, St Kitts, mimeo, 2 July 1991; and 'Time to Act', presentation at the Special Conference of CARICOM Heads of Government to consider the Report of the West Indian Commission, Port of Spain, mimeo, 28 October 1992.

23   Ramphal, 'Time to Act'.

24   Ibid.

25   Ibid.

26   S Ramphal, *'The Negotiations: Process and Preparations'*, presentation to Free Trade Area of the Americas seminar for the Bahamas Public and Private Sector, Nassau, mimeo, 6 March 1998.

27   S Ramphal, *'The West Indian Society: A Recipe for Strength and Growth'*, opening address to the 17th Caribbean Insurance Conference on Securing Our Future, Bridgetown, mimeo, 2 June 1997.

28   Ramphal, *'The Negotiations'*.

29   Ramphal, *Caribbean Alternatives*, p. 10.

30   S Ramphal, 'Address by the Commonwealth Secretary-General on the occasion of the conferment of the Honorary Degree of Doctor of Laws at the University of the West Indies', St Augustine, Trinidad, mimeo, 28 January 1978.

The Commonwealth
context, 1975-1990

— ∞ —

Thatcher and Ramphal: a long and turbulent relationship

Derek Ingram

— ∞ —

Margaret Thatcher's Commonwealth experience was long and often stormy. Only three months after becoming Britain's first woman prime minister she stepped down apprehensively into Lusaka airport, Zambia, on 30 July 1979 for one of the most fraught, and in the end most successful, of all Commonwealth Heads of Government Meetings (CHOGMs). At that point she had little experience of foreign affairs and had been to Africa only once – on a visit to apartheid South Africa as education minister.

It was the first of six Commonwealth summits (plus the special review summit of 1986) she was to attend. Throughout that period Sonny Ramphal was Secretary-General and throughout that period Africa was top of the agenda. The focus was first on the end of white rule in Rhodesia and then on the end of white rule in South Africa. Thatcher's inclinations always leaned towards support for the white position, and this was sustained over the years by pillow talk at No 10. Her husband Denis was instinctively to the right of her, and he also had many longstanding and close business associations with South Africa.

The run-up to Lusaka had been particularly rough. One worry was the question of the Queen's presence, which was by now becoming a regular feature of CHOGM. Not only was the meeting itself expected to be a difficult one; just weeks before CHOGM was due to open the Rhodesians had more than once raided across the border into Zambia, where Joshua Nkomo's ZAPU guerrillas were based. Fears for the safety of the Queen were mixed with Thatcher's own instinct that the

— ∞ —

Derek Ingram, doyen of Commonwealth journalism and founder of the Commonwealth Journalists Association, was editor of the Gemini News Service throughout the period Ramphal was Secretary-General.

royal presence could also distract attention from her own. Thatcher was inclined at first to advise the Queen not to go, but for Commonwealth matters the Queen does not take advice only from the British prime minister. As Head of the Commonwealth she also consults other member governments, and especially in the case of CHOGM the host country and chair. President Kenneth Kaunda of Zambia was particularly anxious that the Queen should attend and she decided she would go. For the Commonwealth it turned out to be a wise decision. Thatcher says in her autobiography that she advised the Queen to go ahead "shortly before the start" of her African tour.

As soon as the Queen arrived in Lusaka for a state visit in advance of the Heads of Government – as was now the custom – she was given a huge welcome, and as she travelled around the Zambian capital and other areas of the country Zambians turned out in their tens of thousands. As a result a better atmosphere was created in advance of the summit, even though Britain's bilateral relations with Zambia and its president had passed through years of strain because of London's failure to take a tough enough stand against the regime in Salisbury. The Zambia *Daily Mail* called the prime minister a racist in contrast with the Queen's "extraordinary loving heart."

Thatcher's arrival was thus overshadowed by the royal visit and this compounded her worries about the meeting. When the prime minister – never quite as "iron" as she was labelled – walked from the plane in Lusaka she was near to tears. During the flight her Foreign and Commonwealth Secretary, Lord Carrington had noticed that, although the landing was to be in darkness, she was carrying a pair of dark glasses. When he asked her why she replied "I am absolutely certain that when I land... they are going to throw acid in my face."

Thatcher knew she was likely to have few sympathisers around the Commonwealth table. Even her right-wing Australian political opposite number, Malcolm Fraser, whose Liberal Party advisers had only a few months earlier helped the British Conservative Party election campaign, had sent two emissaries to 10 Downing Street a day after her election victory to deliver a personal warning. Fraser's message to the new British prime minister was that he would not support her in Lusaka if she continued to favour the Ian Smith-Bishop Abel

Muzorewa government that had been recently voted in by a restricted electorate in Rhodesia. While still in opposition Thatcher had sent an observer group for the elections, which was led by former colonial secretary Lord Boyd. It found that the poll was "fairly conducted and above reproach" and she threatened to recognise it. Carrington strongly opposed hasty recognition of Muzorewa and sent his own envoy, former ambassador to Washington Lord Harlech, to look at the wider situation – namely, that powers such as control of the forces, judiciary and public service, were still firmly in white hands.

All this pre-CHOGM pressure on Thatcher worked. Her speech at the opening ceremony in Lusaka was more constructive and conciliatory than had been anticipated. She in fact laid out a proposal that was to lead within a year, after much hard bargaining and tough talking, to the end of the 15-year-old UDI government and decade-long war, the Lancaster House talks, and the independence of Zimbabwe.

The initiators of this success were Fraser and the prime minister of Jamaica, Michael Manley, but the overall architect of it all was Sonny Ramphal, although the British government and Carrington in particular subsequently did all it could to diminish his role.

Fraser, the right-wing patrician farmer, and Manley, then a far left socialist, were an odd couple. Their first Commonwealth summit had been in 1977 in London. There they discovered they had much in common. At first sight Jamaica and Australia would seem to be countries poles apart, but the two prime ministers found they were on the same side in the global economic arguments then raging. The Caribbean countries and Australia were all commodity producers and suffered from the fixing of world prices by the US and Western Europe, notably in London. In the last days of December 1978 Manley convened an economic summit in Kingston to which he invited Fraser (as well as heavyweights like the German Chancellor Helmut Schmidt). There, in the margins of the meeting, the two took the opportunity to discuss how at the forthcoming CHOGM they might help to break the deadlock over Rhodesia and end the war there. In the months that followed they enlisted, among others, the support of Ramphal and Kaunda, as well as Presidents Nyerere of Tanzania and Samora Machel of Mozambique.

There are few better examples of the value of the Commonwealth as an international forum than this unlikely linkage of Manley and Fraser. These two leaders of opposite political persuasions and from regions on opposite sides of the world might never have met if their countries had not been members of the Commonwealth, certainly not on such informal terms.

At CHOGM in Lusaka the Retreat formula, invented by Canadian prime minister Pierre Trudeau in 1973, came into play, although because of the security situation the leaders had to stay in Lusaka and withdraw to Kaunda's study in State House for their weekend Retreat. There they thrashed out proposals that led to the Lancaster House conference.

The British hoped that the news would not be released for another 48 hours so that Thatcher had time to explain to the media back home why she had done a U-turn. However, Fraser and others feared that unless the deal was quickly made public Heads could start nitpicking, and it would begin to unravel. Fraser leaked details to the Australian press on the Sunday afternoon. Thatcher was furious. At evensong in Lusaka Cathedral she and Ramphal exchanged frantically scribbled notes during the Archbishop's long sermon and between reading a lesson each. They agreed the deal must now be published straight away. At a barbecue in Fraser's villa later in the evening Heads agreed that the details must be released straight away. Owen Harries, adviser to Fraser, described years later how Thatcher broke down in tears at the party over the leakage.

This CHOGM ended on an upbeat note with the famous dinner at which Kaunda and Thatcher danced together. Despite their many disputes in the years that followed, Kaunda to this day still refers to her as "my dancing partner."

Before the Lancaster House talks opened on 10 September Ken Flower, director-general of intelligence in Salisbury, wrote in his diary: "Have I been too pushing with the Bishop? Should we have relied on what Lord Carrington and Co told us in London – that the main purpose of the exercise was 'to see the Bishop confirmed in office as Prime Minister of a moderate, pro-Western government,' when the later news out in London is that Maggie Thatcher actually changed course – was not just veering in the wind... during the Lusaka Conference and is now ready to sacrifice the Bishop in order to please Nyerere, Kaunda and Co. Exactly what I warned them in London last May would happen if they were ill-advised enough to try and get a fair settlement of the Rhodesia problem with Nyerere in on the act."

The exhausting negotiation in Lancaster House, skilfully presided over by Carrington and the Lord Privy Seal, Sir Ian (later Lord) Gilmour, often came near to collapse, with frequent walkout threats. At one point Ramphal warned that the way in which the conference was proceeding was not "within the letter or in the spirit of the Lusaka agreement." – a statement he did not make without knowing that it was the general view of the Commonwealth. Carrington publicly rebuked the Secretary-General, but messages from Nyerere and Kaunda confirmed the Ramphal position.

Ramphal worked tirelessly and successfully to keep Mugabe and Nkomo at the table, enlisting the support of Kaunda, Nyerere and Machel as well as Fraser and Manley. Carrington, with an untypical lack of charity, has always claimed for himself all the credit for the success of Lancaster House. In his biography he mentions Ramphal only once, and then dismissively, saying that he had to keep him "from interfering." He adds that Ramphal "was totally committed to the Patriotic Front, he had no credibility as an impartial observer." The reality is that without his "interfering" the talks might well have collapsed. His job, after all, was to reflect the thinking of all the Commonwealth members, not just of one of them.

All along the British agenda was to keep Mugabe out of power in a new Zimbabwe. No 10 hoped for a coalition of Joshua Nkomo and Bishop Muzorewa, and even up to shortly before the election in February 1980, Thatcher and her ministers seemed to convince themselves that Mugabe would not win. On the ground the evidence was otherwise. One of the toughest tussles with Carrington at Lancaster House had been over the decision to send a Commonwealth observer group for the election. He resisted the idea, wanting not a Commonwealth team but several groups from individual member countries – Australia, Canada and so forth. Ramphal insisted on a single group and he won, although some separate country groups were still sent. The next tussle came when Ramphal rightly insisted that the observers should be on the ground as early as possible. Carrington wanted them to come in at a late stage. In fact,

Ramphal ensured that they started arriving soon after Christmas, and all this compounded Carrington's irritation with him.

When the Commonwealth team led by the shrewd and long-experienced Indian diplomat Rajeshwar Dayal got around the country it became clear to its members that Mugabe was going to win. The British Governor Lord Soames, who moved before the Lancaster House talks ended, and his senior Foreign Office adviser, the realistic Sir Anthony Duff, quite soon recognised that the observers were right. Although there was certainly considerable intimidation, Mugabe was plainly seen as the hero of the liberation struggle by the majority Shona people and Joshua Nkomo's Ndebele were far too thin on the ground. Thatcher says wrongly in her autobiography that Mugabe won "to most people's surprise."

In a last-ditch attempt to keep Mugabe out General Peter Walls, commander of the Smith-Muzorewa regime's forces, appealed to Thatcher to annul the election result.

After Rhodesia finally came off the Commonwealth agenda with independence in 1980 South Africa was to dominate CHOGM discussions for the rest of the decade. From the outset Thatcher dug in her heels. She was happy to go along with the repeated condemnation of apartheid, but the imposition and toughening of sanctions that was to be the central argument of those years was another matter. At every CHOGM she fought a rearguard action and this often brought her into headlong conflict with Ramphal who as Secretary-General was, as always, dutybound to reflect the majority view of Commonwealth member countries, although he had never hidden his own personal views about South Africa. If the Commonwealth was to be true to itself, he said, "it has no option but to be in the vanguard of the final push against apartheid."

Thatcher attended every CHOGM held during her eleven years in office. She never threatened to boycott or walk out but stood her corner, always with plenty to say and rarely missing a session. She was not afraid if almost everyone in the room disagreed with her, as they usually did. As she once told a TV reporter: "If I were the odd one out and I were right that would not matter, would it?" In that sense, Thatcher was not really much in tune with the Commonwealth way of working --

consensus. She never liked what she often referred to as a "fudge". Yet usually in the end after a long fight, she did accept a compromise.

Although Ramphal's relations with Thatcher could sometimes be tense, he always respected her as one who would argue fervently, but would also listen. She sat through as many discussions as possible, in sharp contrast with the other British former prime minister who was in office nearly as long as she was – Tony Blair. He was always restless and impatient, and often gave the impression that he wished he was somewhere else and not having to spend time listening to the views of heads of small states and others he saw as minor players. Thatcher's style was quite different.

As South Africa became increasingly central to the Commonwealth, she became more isolated on the sanctions issue. Just before the Melbourne CHOGM of 1981 Ramphal said in a speech in London that "it is not possible to be an ally of South Africa and a friend of Africa. No one must then be surprised if Africa chooses other friends."

In Melbourne, however, Thatcher was uncharacteristically in somewhat lower key. The headline-stealer there was New Zealand prime minister Robert Muldoon, who was accused of reneging on the Commonwealth sporting links agreement to which he had been a party at Gleneagles in 1977. A Springbok rugby team had just been allowed to tour New Zealand and Ramphal said the Muldoon government had not done enough to stop the tour. At a briefing Muldoon told journalists that "the Secretary should stick to taking the minutes."

In Melbourne Thatcher's rapport with teetotaller Kaunda had continued when, in proposing a toast, he said his only one complaint about the Commonwealth was that "it is dominated by women." He called Thatcher "the beautiful blonde who came and conquered all men." She giggled.

This was the first CHOGM to be attended by Mrs Gandhi, with whom Thatcher had begun to strike up a good relationship. Unlike her father, Jawaharlal Nehru, or her son Rajiv, Gandhi had not at first shown herself to be much of a Commonwealth enthusiast, believing it to be just a useful talking shop. Her views mellowed somewhat and in 1980 she hosted a regional Commonwealth summit and then in Melbourne offered New Delhi for the 1983 CHOGM. By now India was chair of the Non-Aligned Movement.

In Delhi, Thatcher and Gandhi were joined by a third strong woman leader, prime minister Eugenia Charles of Dominica. On the face of it, Ramphal needed all his diplomatic skills. Politically Thatcher was poles apart from Gandhi on South Africa. They were agreed on the immediate issue – the withdrawal of South African troops from southern Angola and the independence of Namibia (then Southwest Africa) – but disagreed on the imposition of economic sanctions against South Africa. Ever since its independence in 1947 India had not even had diplomatic relations with South Africa and never traded with it.

There was now a third unexpected issue. Only five weeks before the Delhi CHOGM, American troops had invaded Grenada following the overthrow and assassination of prime minister Maurice Bishop. The British did not favour American intervention, but Eugenia Charles, as chair of the Organisation of East Caribbean States and now being dubbed the Iron Lady of the Caribbean, flew to Washington to support President Ronald Reagan's decision to invade. In a rare difference, Thatcher was furious with Reagan because he had not forewarned her. Nor had the Queen, Grenada's head of state, been informed. As so often happens at CHOGMs, a sudden issue dominated the meeting. Thatcher and Gandhi found themselves on the same side. Ramphal wanted a Commonwealth civilian presence in place of the US forces. In the communiqué the Heads merely looked forward to a Grenada free of "the presence of foreign military forces", although Gandhi said she had wanted stronger language. However, a positive outcome was the decision to set up a Commonwealth expert group to look at the problems of small states. And it led the Commonwealth to adopt a special role, which continues to this day, on the future of small states.

At the Delhi CHOGM, Ramphal was elected for a third term as secretary-general. Thatcher was by now more than ever at odds with almost all her other Commonwealth colleagues in their increasing pressure for the imposition of economic sanctions on South Africa and Ramphal's duty in his position as SG was as always to articulate the consensus view. Nonetheless, Thatcher supported his re-election and rejected suggestions that he should be given half a five-year term (there was at that time no limit on the number of terms a Secretary-General could serve). The two very different personalities from quite unrelated backgrounds, although both had qualified as lawyers, retained a good working relationship. Ramphal was both diplomat and politician with patience and charm, and after the Lusaka experience he appreciated that Thatcher was conscientious in her attention to the Commonwealth, had always done her homework, and sat through the sessions whenever possible.

But the going got tougher as the Commonwealth's political agenda increasingly concentrated on South Africa. Ramphal had said in his pre-CHOGM biennial report to Heads that it would be unthinkable that any Commonwealth country should offer comfort to South Africa at this time. The 1985 CHOGM was in Bahamas and the always sunny Sonny Ramphal said on arrival in Nassau: "Commonwealth conferences have a long record of turbulence and tempestuousness, but a record of achievement and consensus." It was a fair forecast.

The meeting was marked, as has so often happened at CHOGMs, with a drama. Two days after it opened, and despite clemency calls from the leaders and many parts of the world, sparetime poet and ANC supporter Benjamin Moloise was hanged in Pretoria for killing a policeman. On the same day President P.W. Botha said South Africa would not allow itself to be externally pressured into reform. But events underlined the need for further pressure to be put on South Africa.

Before Indian prime minister Rajiv Gandhi arrived in Nassau he had exchanged correspondence on the sanctions issue with Thatcher. When asked if he was satisfied with her arguments he said: "Not at all. These are the sort of reasons Britain gave to all the countries for not giving them independence when we were under British rule. It's better for you, they said. You're not capable of doing it."

So now Thatcher found herself, more than ever, virtually isolated on the sanctions issue. Ramphal strove to steer the summit into proposals that she would find tolerable and all could accept. Four leaders, Bob Hawke of Australia, Brian Mulroney of Canada, Gandhi and Kaunda, kept meeting her with compromise proposals, but she turned them all down because they contained sanctions. At one point Heads told

Thatcher they would issue their own declaration, but then she gave some ground and agreed to a Commonwealth Accord on Southern Africa setting out what were termed measures, not sanctions, against South Africa. In fact, the list was rather more substantial. It included bans on new government loans to South Africa, the sale and export of oil and computer equipment, a stop on the import of Krugerrands, and an end to government funding for trade missions to South Africa.

Immediately after Thatcher had agreed to the package she gave a press conference at which she claimed that "they joined me" and called her concessions "tiny....tiny", holding a thumb and forefinger only an inch apart. New Zealand prime minister David Lange remarked tartly that "one man's 'sanctions' is another woman's 'measures.'"

The most important outcome of Nassau was the decision to set up the Eminent Persons Group (EPG), which went to South Africa and talked to Nelson Mandela and President P.W. Botha and other members of the Pretoria government. The idea for the EPG came from Australian Prime Minister Bob Hawke and was worked out at the Retreat in Lyford Cay resort. It fitted with Thatcher's insistence that any package of measures on South Africa must include a plan for negotiation that might bring together all the races. Thatcher had gone to Nassau expecting that she would have one or two friends, but in the end she was again totally isolated. Even Malawi and Swaziland gave her no real support.

The EPG was led by Malcolm Fraser and Olusegun Obasanjo, both then out of office, and produced the historic report *Mission to South Africa* that set out proposals for a negotiating concept for constitutional change and a transfer to democratic government. Eventually, these hugely contributed to the settlement reached between the F.W. de Klerk government and the ANC and other parties, ending apartheid and leading to Mandela's accession to power – a Commonwealth contribution that to this day has been greatly underrated. It was the first international political breakthrough on South Africa after decades of pressure and arguably one of the Commonwealth's most important achievements, even though eight more years were to pass before the end of apartheid was finally achieved.

In Nassau Thatcher had agreed at the retreat in Lyford Cay to the concept of the mission, but as soon as she returned to London she argued about its composition. She wanted her Foreign and Commonwealth Secretary, Sir Geoffrey Howe, to lead the group while Ramphal and other Heads saw it as being made up not of government ministers or officials but of persons who would be acting in their personal capacities. It was one of the lowest points in Ramphal-Thatcher relations. In the end Thatcher gave way and nominated as the British member Lord Barber, who had been a Conservative Chancellor of the Exchequer (in the government of Edward Heath) and was now chairman of the Standard Chartered Bank.

Thatcher ensured, however, that Howe did visit South Africa. He went independently as President of the Council of Ministers of the EEC (now European Union) after the EPG mission and a month before the Commonwealth held a review meeting in London of seven Heads in August 1986.

At the time the EPG looked like a failure because before the mission had finished its job South Africa launched a series of cross-border raids and Ramphal pulled the team out early. Thatcher thought it was a wrong decision and that it should have gone on talking to the South Africans. At one point in her autobiography Thatcher refers to the EPG as "a fiasco," which it was nothing of the sort. She also suspected Ramphal of trying to encourage Commonwealth leaders to take measures against Britain if she did not now support further sanctions.

The review meeting was held in London and brought together seven heads, most of whom had hosted CHOGMs – Sir Lynden Pindling (Bahamas), who was in the chair, Bob Hawke (Australia) Brian Mulroney (Canada), Thatcher, Rajiv Gandhi, Kaunda and Mugabe. Here again Thatcher would not budge on backing all the sanctions the rest of the Commonwealth wanted, but said she would put voluntary bans on new investment and tourism and accept any EEC decision to ban imports of coal, iron, steel and gold coins. For the first time the cherished Commonwealth tradition of consensus was broken and the communiqué contained a paragraph putting the separate British position on sanctions. At the time commentators saw it as the toughest time of Ramphal's career. The British accused him of writing a preface to the report which called more forthrightly for sanctions than did the EPG report itself.

The Thatcher attitude to South Africa unleashed a stream of attack on the Commonwealth in the British press in mid-1986 that was reminiscent of what had happened in the aftermath of Ian Smith's UDI in 1965. Rupert Murdoch's *The Sun* pointed in a leading article on the Commonwealth to the Queen's "natural interest in retaining as many members as possible," adding "but who cares if every single black nation walks out."

At the next CHOGM held in Vancouver (1987) the consensus was broken again and more overtly. Thatcher was at her most combative. As the apartheid years neared their end repression, cross-border raids and the worsening situation in Namibia intensified. Most Commonwealth leaders were increasingly frustrated by Thatcher's stand on sanctions. She fought back, accusing them of hypocrisy. She argued that some African countries were economically dependent on South Africa, could not implement sanctions themselves, and wanted others to do their dirty work. The Commonwealth was now seriously divided. This time the communiqué paragraphs on South Africa were prefaced five times by the phrase "with the exception of Britain." To make matters worse, four leaders – Hawke, Kaunda, Gandhi and Mugabe – called a press conference to denounce Britain for conducting "a process of disinformation to some extent, or misinformation" about the talks. Thatcher promptly held a separate press conference during which she referred to the ANC as a "typical terrorist organisation."

This greatly upset the Foreign and Commonwealth Office whose junior minister Lynda Chalker and officials had recently begun to engage ANC President Oliver Tambo and other leaders in talks in London. Chalker had done so without Thatcher's agreement and was duly carpeted by the prime minister. One major decision in Vancouver Britain did not support was the setting up of a Committee of Foreign Ministers on South Africa (COMSA). Thatcher said the committee would be a waste of time and counter-productive and Britain never joined it, but it proved to be a most useful body as South Africa moved towards ending apartheid and one of Mandela's first acts after his release from 27 years in prison was to attend a meeting of COMSA in Abuja.

Ramphal regards Vancouver as the lowest point in his relationship with Thatcher and the most difficult of all his CHOGMs. Officials drafting the communiqué, with its British exceptions, laboured far into the night.

By the introduction into CHOGM statements of a government's exception to the majority position Thatcher had seemed to be breaking the long-established Commonwealth tradition of consensus. On the eve of the Vancouver meeting Ramphal was asked at a press conference whether he envisioned the Commonwealth moving "towards a situation where it no longer requires a consensus when it takes important decisions." He replied that he did not see the Commonwealth adopting a voting system, but added that "...it carries the important implication that really there will from time to time be matters on which there is such an overwhelming sentiment in the Commonwealth that one particular country standing aside from it, perhaps for the time being, shouldn't frustrate Commonwealth action."

Thatcher still did not mind being apparently isolated. She continued to insist she was right and the remainder wrong and said she was sorry for the others. Nevertheless, she left Vancouver saying that she had had "an easy conference" and that the absence of new sanctions had shown "implicit recognition that further progress cannot be made along these lines." Ramphal took an opposite view, promising that "sanctions will be widened, intensified, universalised. For most of us they are on the front burner." The reality is that over the years Thatcher was slowly forced to give ground, going right back to that first painful experience in Lusaka until she came for her last CHOGM in Kuala Lumpur in 1989, chaired by Mohamad Mahathir. Thatcher had much in common with Mahathir; she describes him in her autobiography as "tough, shrewd and practical...refreshingly matter-of-fact."

She arrived in Malaysia determined as ever to give no ground on sanctions and took up the old arguments with Hawke and Mulroney. The situation in South Africa was now moving along – in a few months de Klerk would replace Botha as state president – and COMSA and most heads round the table argued that now was the time to tighten the screw and strengthen sanctions. Thatcher would still have none of it and once again she objected to the final draft of the communiqué, which her new Foreign and Commonwealth Secretary, John Major, had just approved.

It turned out that there had been a lack of communication between Major and Thatcher and her private secretary Charles Powell. She had asked Powell to draft a second statement, but in the meantime at the

Retreat the leaders had given some ground to Thatcher, of which Major was unaware. Major issued the first statement as a joint statement with the result that the impression was given that Thatcher had signed an agreement at 5 pm and repudiated it at 6 pm. Not a happy experience for the man who was to succeed Thatcher a few months later as prime minister.

Despite some concessions to Thatcher, the Commonwealth's final communiqué called for more sanctions and used the phrase – on this occasion four times – "except for Britain". The main new measures were financial – calling on banks to toughen conditions on trade financing. This was an Australian initiative and turned out to be one of the most effective late pressures on Pretoria. Major says in his autobiography: "I licked my wounds and prepared to be more careful the next time Margaret and I travelled abroad together."

In Kuala Lumpur the bumpy, decade-long relationship between Thatcher and Ramphal came to an end. For both it was their last CHOGM. Ramphal left office in mid-1990. Just four months later Thatcher was forced out as prime minister.

Shridath Ramphal: *Inseparable Humanity*, 1988

Margaret Thatcher: *The Downing Street Years*, 1993

Hugo Young: *One of Us*, 1989

Lord Carrington: *Reflect on Things Past*, 1988

John Major: *The Autobiography*, 1999

Emeka Anyaoku: *The Inside Story of the Modern Commonwealth*, 2004

Robert Harvey: *The Fall of Apartheid*, 2001

Ken Flower: *Serving Secretly*, 1987

David Martin and Phyllis Johnson: *The Struggle for Zimbabwe*, 1981

Gemini News Service reports on 1979-89 CHOGMs

Commonwealth Africa: background to the anti-apartheid struggle

Guy Arnold

— ∞ —

During the momentous years in which Ramphal was Secretary-General, it is understandable that Commonwealth and international attention was mainly focused upon the unfolding developments in southern Africa. The Soweto uprising of 1976 ushered in a new era of confrontation in South Africa, which culminated with President F. W. de Klerk's speech of 2 February 1990 that signalled the coming end of apartheid. In 1980, after 15 years of UDI, Rhodesia became independent as Zimbabwe, an event that could reasonably be described as a Commonwealth triumph, while ten years later Namibia achieved independence from South Africa. As a consequence of this concentration upon the south, events elsewhere in Commonwealth Africa received less attention than they deserved. Yet from Nigeria to Tanzania and Uganda to Zambia major changes were underway and radically different political and economic approaches to development were followed in Nigeria, Tanzania, Ghana and Botswana.

Nigeria had been deeply affected by the OPEC-inspired oil price rises of 1973 so that between 1974 and 1976 the Third National Development Plan was reshaped and expanded several times, as the country embarked upon a period of free spending. This approach to its new oil wealth received a boost when further oil price rises occurred between 1978 and 1981. General Yacubu Gowon's last achievement had been to bring about the formation of the Economic Community of West African States (ECOWAS) in May 1975. Two

— ∞ —

Guy Arnold has written several books about Africa, the most recent being "Africa: a modern history" 2005.

months later, in a bloodless military coup of 29 July, Gowon was replaced as head of state while attending the OAU Summit in Kampala by General Murtala Muhammed. By this time the military had established itself as the central motivator in Nigerian politics.

Muhammed, nicknamed "no nonsense Muhammed", carried through a number of much needed reforms: he sacked most of the state governors for corruption or incompetence, initiated a major drive against corruption, cancelled the 1973 census results which had become a bone of political contention, created seven new states to bring the total to 19 and set 1979 as the date for a return to civilian rule. Muhammed was assassinated on 13 February 1976 in a botched coup attempt led by Lieutenant-Colonel Bukar Dimka. Instead, Muhammed's deputy, Lieutenant-General Olusegun Obasanjo, became head of state and continued with his predecessor's programme of reforms.

In September 1978, the state of emergency that had been imposed in 1966 was finally lifted and a new constitution that allowed political parties to operate again was inaugurated. Elections were held through July and August 1979; these were won by the National Party of Nigeria (NPN) led by Shehu Shagari, who became Nigeria's first executive president. Meanwhile, as the Commonwealth Heads of Government met in Lusaka for the historic conference that led to the end of UDI in Rhodesia, Nigeria nationalised BP (Nigeria) – in its timing a deliberate shot across Prime Minister Margaret Thatcher's bows – on the grounds that BP had broken sanctions against South Africa by landing Nigerian oil in that country earlier in the year.

Nigeria now experienced four troubled years of civilian rule under Shagari. The opposition never accepted the validity of his election victory, economic problems piled up with the end of the oil boom and corruption became endemic to the system. A new problem arose at this time when the popular Muslim preacher, Alhaji Muhammad Marwa (Maitatsine), preached sermons that exacerbated Muslim-Christian antagonisms in the north of the country. In 1983, a panic reaction to deteriorating economic conditions, the government expelled two million foreign workers, the majority from Ghana, in a move that hurt Nigeria's standing in West Africa while doing little to resolve its economic problems. In the elections of 1983 Shagari and the NPN won a second term but in a deeply divided nation whose people had not been persuaded of the fairness of the Federal solution to Nigeria's politics.

The result was predictable, and on 31 December the army stepped in under Maj.-Gen. Muhammed Buhari to dismiss the civilian government and return the country to military rule. Buhari, however, failed to solve Nigeria's economic problems and was himself replaced in another coup of 1985 that brought Major-General Ibrahim Babangida to power. He promised to return the country to civilian rule in 1989, but this did not happen.

The 1970s were a dismal decade for Ghana whose economy was in freefall. It was ruled by an increasingly corrupt military under Lieutenant-Colonel Ignatius Kutu Acheampong. He was replaced in mid-1978 by yet another soldier, General Frederick Akuffo. The country was ripe for change when the populist Flight-Lieutenant Jerry Rawlings led junior officers and NCOs in a coup attempt on 15 May 1979. The coup failed and Rawlings was imprisoned. But three weeks later on 4 June his followers released him from prison, to establish an Armed Forces Revolutionary Council; Rawlings became effective head of state.

Later in June three former military heads of state – Afrifa, Acheampong and Akuffo – were executed. Rawlings then allowed elections that had already been scheduled for July to proceed and these were won by the People's National Party led by Hilla Limann who was elected President in September. Limann, a former academic, was never a convincing head of state and in any case owed his position to Rawlings and the military who became a de facto last court of appeal. This civilian government collapsed at the end of 1981 and on 31 December Rawlings resumed power.

This time round he launched a programme of mass democratisation and mass participation, an experiment in people's power or grassroots socialism under the auspices of a Provisional National Defence Council (1982-1984). Rawlings' ideas of people's power met with much opposition in what was essentially a conservative society. By the mid 1980s, reacting to world economic realities,

Rawlings turned to orthodox economic methods and adopted a recovery programme endorsed by the World Bank and IMF, with the result that Ghana experienced an economic revival in the latter half of the 1980s.

In Sierra Leone, anti-government demonstrations in 1977 persuaded President Siaka Stevens to seek support in the House of Representatives for a one-party constitution. He obtained a majority for this in 1978, which was later confirmed by referendum. The opposition Sierra Leone People's Party (SLPP) then joined the ruling All People's Congress. However, as with much of Africa during the 1980s, Sierra Leone experienced steady economic decline accompanied by growing opposition to the rule of Siaka Stevens.

Stevens was forced to step down in 1985 in favour of Major-General Joseph Saida Momoh. By April 1989, the 28th anniversary of independence, Sierra Leone appeared to be in permanent economic crisis: its refineries were only operating at 40 per cent capacity due to lack of oil to process; its alluvial diamonds and gold produced little revenue since they were regularly smuggled out of the country; and in 1990 the Leone currency was devalued. By the end of that year an increasing flow of refugees from the civil war in neighbouring Liberia foreshadowed the coming civil war in Sierra Leone itself, which would last for a decade.

By 1980 in The Gambia, Sir Dawda Jawara had been president of the country for a decade, and there was growing opposition to his rule and that of the People's Progressive Party. Two new parties emerged – the Gambia Socialist Revolutionary Party (GSRP) and the Movement for Justice in Africa – Gambia (MOJA-G). Both were advocating extreme anti-government measures. Following the murder of the deputy leader of the paramilitary field force, Jawara called upon Senegal for assistance and his neighbour sent 150 troops to safeguard the president and forestall a possible coup. The two opposition parties were then proscribed.

The Gambia, in any case, was a geographical anomaly and, without the Scramble for Africa would have been part of Senegal. A more serious attempt to overthrow the government was mounted in July 1981 when Jawara was on a visit to India. The rebels, led by Kukoi

Samba Sanyang, took control of key points in Banjul, issued arms indiscriminately, and released convicts from the prison. There was widespread violence. Jawara flew back to Dakar and this time obtained far greater assistance from Senegal in the form of 3,000 troops, which were despatched to The Gambia. In the fighting that followed their arrival, 1,000 lives were lost and another 1,000 dissidents were detained under emergency regulations.

The Senegalese troops were to remain in The Gambia throughout the 1980s and posed an intriguing problem for the tiny state. In 1982 the two countries created a Confederation of Senegambia. But by 1989 – like so many other moves towards union in Africa – the arrangement had broken down and, following the withdrawal of Senegal's troops, the confederation was dissolved in September. In February 1990 The Gambia celebrated 25 years of independence.

During the 1980s the three Commonwealth countries of East Africa – Kenya, Uganda and Tanzania – faced comparable economic problems to those of West Africa while Uganda suffered years of violence following the overthrow of Idi Amin in 1979. Jomo Kenyatta, the architect of Kenyan independence died peacefully in his bed in 1978 and was accorded a grand funeral in Nairobi that was attended by many African heads of state. Kenyatta was succeeded, after a brilliant eight-week campaign that was stage-managed on his behalf by the Attorney-General Charles Njonjo, by Vice-President Daniel arap Moi, who coined the term Nyayo (footsteps) to indicate he would follow his predecessor's policies.

By 1980, the honeymoon that he had enjoyed on coming to power was over and Moi was subjected to increasing criticism in the national assembly and from students. In August 1982 the air force mounted a coup attempt in Nairobi where key installations and buildings were seized and held for a day before the army and the General Service Unit (GSU) regained control. Official figures gave the death toll as 159 though unofficial estimates put the figure much higher, while 2,000 air force personnel and 1,000 citizens were detained. In the end 14 of the plotters were executed.

By 1983 Moi saw Charles Njonjo, the "kingmaker" who had ensured that he got the presidency, as too popular and influential.

So he had him accused of working as a "stooge" for foreign powers and disgraced. Though he was then pardoned, his political career was finished. In 1986 Moi greatly increased his presidential powers when control of the civil service was transferred to the President's Office. Two years later the ruling Kenya African National Union (KANU) won the 1988 elections though known opponents of the president such as Oginga Odinga were barred from standing. Moi was re-elected president for the third time. He then demoted his popular vice-president, Mwai Kibaki. In 1989 Odinga became reconciled to Moi and called upon all Kenyans to support the government. In May the vice-president Josephat Karanja was accused by party leaders of arrogance and forced to resign before being expelled from KANU.

The pattern was a familiar one: politicians who became too influential were forced out of office. In June Moi allowed all political prisoners to be released. He attacked the Daily Nation for its political reporting and Arab countries for opposing his decision to resume diplomatic relations with Israel. By the end of the decade there were growing demands for a return to multi-party politics. In February 1990 the highly able Foreign Minister, Robert Ouku, was killed, a political murder that did great damage to Kenya's image. By this time Moi was demonstrating all the traits of a dictator.

In Uganda, support for Idi Amin evaporated between 1976 and 1979. In 1978 Amin launched an attack upon Tanzania through the Kagera salient in which he placed troops of doubtful loyalty in the front and then had them massacred from behind. In January 1979 the Tanzanian army and Ugandan exiles of Yoweri Museveni's National Liberation Army invaded Uganda; Kampala was occupied over 10-11 April and Amin fled the country.

The defeat of Amin did not bring an end to Uganda's troubles. Milton Obote, who had been ousted by Amin in 1971 while he was attending the Singapore CHOGM to support Kaunda and Nyerere in their determination to oppose the newly elected government of Edward Heath selling arms to South Africa, now made a comeback. His Uganda People's Congress (UPC) won 68 of 126 seats in the election of 1980, which, however, was widely regarded as rigged, with the result that Museveni's Uganda Patriotic Movement that had contested the election, now took to the bush and built up its National Resistance Army (NRA).

Violence in 1981 and 1982 escalated dramatically in 1983. Tens of thousands of Ugandans became refugees, many of them being targeted by the army which was out of control. By 1985, as the economic recovery faltered, Museveni's NRA launched an offensive. In July the army mounted a coup and Obote fled to Zambia. A military Council was formed under General Tito Okello and this appointed Paulo Muwango (Obote's vice-president) as prime minister.

The appointment was a cause of anger to the NRA, and this was further increased when the army began to recruit former Amin soldiers. The NRA launched a lightning campaign at the beginning of 1986 to capture Kampala. Museveni was sworn in as President although there was continuing violence for several more years. In October 1989 Museveni announced that democratic elections and a return to civilian rule would be delayed until 1995. Through the Amin years, and on to the end of the 1980s when Museveni had established full control, Uganda had suffered huge casualties. It is estimated that 300,000 were killed during Amin's period in power, and a further 500,000 died during the fighting of the 1980s.

In Tanzania the ruling party, TANU, was replaced in 1976 by a single revolutionary party to include the mainland and Zanzibar, Chama Cha Mapundizi. In October the Chinese built the TANZAM railway covering 1167 miles between Dar es Salaam and Kapiri Mposhi in Zambia was completed. It was a symbol of the two countries' determination to break away from western tutelage and dependence upon transit routes through the white-controlled south. The railway was not welcomed in the West.

President Julius Nyerere's experiment in cooperative socialism – ujamaa villages – reached its apogee in 1979 when 8,000 villages (90 per cent of mainland villages) had established their own governments in the form of village assemblies. The following year Nyerere was re-elected president for the fifth time winning 93 per cent of the votes cast. He announced that he would not stand again in 1985. However, economic decline during the decade brought a growing realisation that the ujamaa programme of villageisation had not worked, in part

As Guyana's Foreign Minister, Ramphal had worked hard for Caribbean integration. This signed commemorative picture (Michael Manley five from R) marks the decision of Caribbean leaders in 1972 to establish the Caribbean Community (CARICOM). It was followed a year later by the Treaty of Chaguaramas, signed in Trinidad and Tobago

Ramphal and compatriot Clive Lloyd, former West Indies Cricket Captain, receive honorary degrees from Hull University in 1984 on the 150th anniversary of the abolition of slavery

The new Secretary-General, with his predecessor, Arnold Smith of Canada, conversing in the conference room of Marlborough House, 1975

Escorting the Queen, Head of the Commonwealth, at Ramphal's first Commonwealth Day reception in May 1976. The Queen has made time to attend these receptions every year

Ramphal's first Heads of Government Meeting as Secretary-General was in London in 1977 under the chairmanship of Prime Minister James Callaghan, above, walking to Lancaster House with Archbishop Makarios of Cyprus

With Prime Minister Pierre Trudeau of Canada (second from R), at the Gleneagles Retreat of the 1977 Commonwealth Heads of Government Meeting – with Audrey Callaghan and Lois Ramphal (first and second from L)

To Sonny – with warm thanks and every good wish.

Margaret   Lusaka '79

Despite early misgivings, Prime Minister Margaret Thatcher was pleased with the outcome of the Commonwealth Heads' Meeting in Lusaka in 1979 – and signed this photo was "warm thanks" to Ramphal afterwards. At subsequent meetings she was often out of step with her colleagues and the Secretary-General over South Africa

Ramphal with Prime Minister Indira Gandhi, 1980, shortly after she was returned to office [NB picture to be taken from "Inseparable Humanity"]

Five leaders who chaired Commonwealth summits in a Melbourne garden, 1981: L to R, President Kaunda (1979) and Prime Ministers Malcolm Fraser (1981), Indira Gandhi (1983), Lee Kuan Yew (1971) and Pierre Trudeau (1973)

A moment of relaxation at the Retreat weekend of the Melbourne summit, 1981. President Kaunda and Prime Ministers Trudeau and Ratu Mara (Fiji) enjoy a round of golf with kangaroo escorts

At the annual Blenheim Palace cricket match between the Foreign and Commonwealth Office and the Commonwealth Secretariat, Foreign Secretary Sir Geoffrey Howe receives the prize – his wife Lady Elspeth Howe had made the top score

With the Duke of Edinburgh on the occasion of his wedding anniversary. Ramphal joked with Prince Philip that he had arrived in London as a student in 1947 on the day of the Royal Wedding, mistaking the banners as a welcome

As Foreign Minister of Guyana, Ramphal presides over the UN Security Council in 1975, shortly before becoming Commonwealth Secretary-General

The Brundtland Commission played a seminal role in the environment debate. Ramphal (L) stands next to Gro-Harlem Brundtland in a meeting of the commission with its secretariat, Oslo, 1985

With Willy Brandt at the launch of the Willy Brandt Foundation, which took forward the ideas of the Brandt Commission

With Lord Scarman, who undertook an inquiry into race riots in Britain, after receiving an honorary degree from Warwick University in 1988. A year later Ramphal succeeded Scarman as Chancellor of the university

because the bureaucracy had been unable to supply the necessary support. Increasing shortages of consumer goods and lack of foreign exchange became acute.

In October 1985, as he had promised, Nyerere stood down to be succeeded as president by Ali Hassan Mwinyi. After an initial period in which he made only minimal policy changes, Mwinyi inaugurated a major policy shift when he accepted IMF proposals for economic restructuring, thus signalling the end of Nyerere's experiment in grass roots socialism. Tanzania now moved back into mainstream orthodox western-style economics. Even so, Nyerere had made a unique impact upon Tanzania and Africa and, though his socialist policy had failed, he had created a moral and social climate that stood out in a continent where political self-serving was too often the norm.

As Mwinyi liberalised the economy a rift developed between him and Nyerere who had remained chairman of Chama Cha Mapundizi and opposed any dealings with the IMF. However, with typical generosity, Nyerere acknowledged Mwinyi's success in tightening up the administration and said he had made "the new government look like a government." In February 1990, Nyerere – the architect and intellectual defender of the one-party state – said publicly that Tanzania should consider multi-party politics again. Later in the year Nyerere resigned as chairman of Chama Cha Mapundizi, in favour of Mwinyi.

During the Ramphal years Mauritius favoured a multi-party system and enjoyed economic progress and political stability. Seychelles, the other Indian Ocean Commonwealth island territory, became a one-party state in 1979 under Albert Rene and the Seychelles People's Progressive Front (SPPF).

All the countries of Central and Southern Africa were drawn, to a greater or lesser extent, into the events that led to independence for Rhodesia as Zimbabwe after 15 years of UDI and the end of apartheid in South Africa ten years later. Zambia played a vital role as a frontline state, and President Kenneth Kaunda was a leading player. On the home front, Zambia suffered as a landlocked country that was overwhelmingly dependent upon rail routes through its southern neighbours for the export of its bulk copper and for imports. A turning point for Zambia came in 1974: after celebrating ten years of independence, when its economic prospects looked bright, the price of copper, its principal foreign exchange earner, collapsed.

By 1978, facing a deepening economic crisis, Zambia was obliged to reopen the rail links through Rhodesia though it continued to support the liberation movements – ZANU and ZAPU – in the final stages of the struggle that led to independence. Both Rhodesia and South Africa put pressure on Zambia with periodic air strikes, as in 1986 when South Africa raided neighbouring states in order to abort the Commonwealth Eminent Persons initiative.

Malawi under Hastings Banda became black Africa's "odd man out" because of the president's decision to open diplomatic relations with South Africa, a policy that he often made a point of flaunting, much to the irritation of the frontline states that were his neighbours. Only when Rhodesia became independent as Zimbabwe in 1980 did the changing scene in southern Africa force Banda to alter his policies. He joined SADCC as a founding member in 1980 and hosted its 1981 annual meeting. Banda's relations with Mozambique had been strained ever since it became independent in 1975 although President Samora Machel visited Malawi in 1984 in an effort to improve understanding between the two countries.

In July 1986, however, Mozambique accused Malawi of assisting the Renamo guerrillas inside Mozambique and the following September Banda denied this accusation at a meeting with Machel, Kaunda and Mugabe held in Malawi. Following the air crash in which Machel lost his life, the South Africans claimed that documents found in the wreckage revealed a plot by Mozambique and Zimbabwe to overthrow the Malawi government. As developments moved towards a climax in South Africa, Malawi became more amenable in its dealings with its neighbours. In 1987, for example, Banda committed 300 troops to assist the Frelimo government of Mozambique and Tanzania to guard the strategic rail link from Nacala on the Indian Ocean through to Blantyre against Renamo attacks. In 1988 Malawi became the unwilling host to more than 650,000 refugees from the civil war in Mozambique.

Throughout the 15 years considered here, Botswana steadily developed its valuable mining sector while resisting South African pressures to enter into a dialogue with the apartheid state. As the Botswana government made plain, it was only prepared to engage in a dialogue that was concerned with the attainment of majority rule. As it developed its mineral wealth – by 1984 diamonds accounted for 76 per cent of exports – Botswana faced a growing problem. It was creating a state divided into two societies. There was a wealthier urban population that largely worked for the mines or the government, and a majority of the people living in the poor rural areas and shanty towns. South African pressure on Botswana escalated during the 1980s and led one of Africa's more conservative governments to purchase arms from the Soviet Union.

President Quett Masire accused the United States of backing the intransigent attitudes of South Africa. In 1982 he warned that South Africa wanted to turn Botswana into another Lebanon. In 1986 Botswana was one of the frontline states to suffer a cross border raid by South Africa, which had determined to scupper the work of the Commonwealth Eminent Persons Group then visiting the republic. Despite such pressures, Botswana had the satisfaction during the second half of the 1980s of seeing its currency, the pula, become stronger than the South African rand.

Lesotho is totally surrounded by South African territory. During this period, it constantly struggled to maintain some form of independence from its giant neighbour. It had almost no resources except labour for the South African mines. During the 1970s President Leabua Jonathan had become increasingly dictatorial with the result that anti-government violence erupted in1978-79. Chief Jonathan's main political opponent was Ntsu Mpkhehle of the Basutoland Congress Party (BCP) who went into exile in South Africa.

From there, Mpkhehle's Lesotho Liberation Army (LLA) launched periodic cross-border attacks upon Lesotho to destabilise Jonathan, an activity that suited Pretoria. Such incursions were carried out in 1978, 1979, 1982 and 1983. Then, at the beginning of 1986 South Africa effectively blockaded Lesotho after Jonathan had refused to agree to a joint security pact or expel members of the ANC. On 20 January 1986, Jonathan was deposed by Major-General Justin Lekhanya and placed under house arrest. He died in April 1987 while in South Africa for medical treatment. He had acted as a constant irritant to South Africa.

Swaziland, landlocked between South Africa and Mozambique, felt obliged to cooperate with South Africa, a policy that suited its reactionary royal family, whose old King, Sobhuza II, had abrogated the constitution and abolished all political parties in 1973 to rule by royal decree. There then followed a large influx of South African capital that came to dominate the economy. In 1978 Swaziland established an indirect electoral system based upon 40 local councils that chose members to attend an electoral college. In reality absolute power remained in the hands of the king.

The country enjoyed close relations with South Africa throughout the 1980s. Following the 1984 Nkomati Accord between South Africa and Mozambique, Swaziland deported 200 members of the ANC to Zambia and Tanzania. In 1985 the Swazi Prime Minister defended the country's close relations with South Africa at the SADCC meeting, which was held in Mbabane. He did the same at the Commonwealth summit in the Bahamas later that year when, alone of member countries, Swaziland supported Margaret Thatcher in her opposition to sanctions against South Africa. Even so, South Africa carried out border raids into Swaziland between 1985 and 1988.

Namibia, or South West Africa, had been a German colony which became a League of Nations mandate handed to South Africa. In December 1976 the UN General Assembly denounced South Africa's repressive measures in the territory. It called on the Security Council to impose mandatory sanctions against the Pretoria government and recognise the justice of the South West African People's Organisation's (SWAPO) military campaign. From this point onwards South Africa backed UNITA in southern Angola so as both to harass the MPLA government in that country and to deny access to Namibia to the SWAPO forces based in Angola.

In September 1978 South Africa announced that it would hold elections in December for a Namibia Constituent Assembly and on 20 September, when it insisted that it would proceed with its own internal settlement, the UN responded by adopting Security Council Resolution 435, which formalised the UN Action Plan on Namibia.

This created a framework for Namibian independence and was followed by the establishment of a UN Transition Assistance Group (UNTAG) to help the Special Representative achieve independence through fair elections. There followed ten years of talks, endless political manoeuvres and the escalation of the conflict in the Caprivi Strip between SWAPO forces and the South African Defence Force (SADF).

Complicating the issue further, US President Ronald Reagan adopted the policy of linking a settlement in Namibia to the withdrawal of Cuban forces from Angola. In 1985 South Africa set up a Transitional Government of National Unity (TGNU) for Namibia. This was widely condemned by the international community, which refused to recognise its validity. By 1986 South Africa admitted that it had 35,000 troops deployed in Namibia. In 1987 the People's Liberation Army of Namibia (PLAN) launched attacks upon white farms. Then in January 1989, reflecting other changes in the region, the UN Security Council adopted a number of resolutions to enable the process set out in Resolution 435 to be activated and set aside a budget for the UN Transition Assistance Group.

On 6 June 1989, President de Klerk of South Africa declared an end to apartheid in Namibia and an amnesty for guerrillas returning from Angola. Elections were held in November, supervised by 1,695 UN-trained personnel and of 700,000 registered voters 90 per cent took part. SWAPO won a clear majority winning 57.3 per cent of the votes cast. Namibia became independent on 21 March 1990 and Sam Nujoma became its first president. Reflecting Commonwealth support for the liberation struggle, the newly independent country joined the Commonwealth.

It is far from easy to quantify the achievements and setbacks that occurred in Commonwealth Africa over these years. After long, sustained pressures, some of the most notable advances took place in the south of the continent: Zimbabwe became independent in 1980; Namibia in 1990, the year in which President de Klerk signalled the end of apartheid in South Africa. A notable success story was that of Botswana, where economic development and a moderate democratic system provided the stability that enabled the government to withstand the many threats and pressures exerted upon it by South Africa.

In the north of the continent, however, the Commonwealth countries of West Africa experienced a decline in democratic standards, the growth of corruption and the pervasive influence of the military. Nigeria, indeed, suffered four military coups in 1975, 1976, 1981 and 1985; in Ghana a decade of increasingly corrupt military rule was terminated by the Rawlings revolution, yet only after this period came to an end did Rawlings move – slowly – to return Ghana to full multiparty democracy again.

Violent ethnic, religious and power differences affected Ghana and Nigeria in West Africa, and Kenya and Uganda in East Africa. Too often the rule of law was flouted by regimes that paid scant attention to democracy, while entrenching the autocratic rule of the head of state and his accompanying elite. The ease with which constitutions and the rule of law could be set aside revealed the structural fragility of most African states.

Above all, it was in the economic sphere that these countries suffered repeated setbacks, partly due to external factors beyond their control, partly the result of mistaken policies. The decade of the 1980s witnessed ever rising debts, unfavourable terms of trade for export commodities, and declining agricultural output. Three decades after independence had been achieved, aid dependency had become a permanent feature of most economies. This encouraged the outside world to view Africa as a series of "basket cases" that needed the World Bank and IMF to mount rescue operations.

In 1979 an OAU symposium produced a document, "What kind of Africa by the Year 2000?", which provided the framework for the Lagos Plan of Action of 1980. The plan called for collective self-reliance and an end to aid dependency. Unfortunately, self-reliance was to remain an aspiration for too many countries through the dismal 1980s while in Tanzania, the collapse of of Nyerere's ujamaa experiment – the continent's most famous attempt at home-grown socialism – signalled one more defeat for African self-reliance.

How to sum up these years? Achievements, too often, were overshadowed by economic or military crises. Yet, slowly, the transition from colonial to real independent status was taking place. The long years of military rule in Nigeria convinced more and more

Nigerians that they had to return to multi-party democracy. The realities of world economics brought an end to revolutionary experiments in Ghana and Tanzania. And though the 1980s saw much flouting of the primary Commonwealth principles of democracy, the rule of law, freedom of the press and greater government transparency, these principles became objectives to be pursued in the next decade. By 1990, the accumulated experience of 30 years of freedom, and an awareness of the relentless pressures Africans faced from outside, produced a growing understanding that real advances could only be achieved from within.

An unlucky Secretary-General: Sonny Ramphal and a 'Season of Caesars' in Commonwealth South Asia

James Manor

— ∞ —

Sonny Ramphal was the sort of international leader who tended to make his own luck. He did his homework, calculated shrewdly, and brought such radiant good humour to his work that unlikely achievements sometimes became possible. But during his time as Secretary-General, no amount of careful preparation and bonhomie could overcome the bad hand that he was dealt in Commonwealth South Asia – the region embracing Bangladesh, India, Pakistan and Sri Lanka.

This is no trivial slice of the Commonwealth. Just one South Asian country – India – contains over half of the population of this association of states and peoples. India, Bangladesh and Pakistan are the Commonwealth's three largest countries. But in Sonny's day – between 1975 and 1990 – they were inward-looking and nearly always poorly governed. If the standards of the Harare Declaration – adopted later, in October 1991 – had been applied to them, all four governments would have qualified at various times, and often for extended periods, for suspension from membership. This handicapped the contribution they could make to the Commonwealth under his stewardship.

This issue has had far less attention than it deserves because the most visible problems afflicting the Commonwealth in that period arose

— ∞ —

James Manor, Emeka Anyaoku Professor of Commonwealth Studies, London University, is author of several books on South Asia.

from southern Africa – from Rhodesia/Zimbabwe and apartheid South Africa. But South Asia offered a quite remarkable array of unappealing, often vile regimes and no shortage of outrages. These need explaining – a painful task, since this writer enjoys nothing more than celebrating South Asian successes – in order to indicate what Sonny, and the Commonwealth that he led, were up against.

It is important to provide a little historical context, and to consider a theme that loomed large in that span of 15 years, but which is sometimes overlooked and almost always underemphasised. Sonny's term as Secretary-General straddles a hugely important transition which created major challenges for leaders of Commonwealth member governments and, to a degree, for the Commonwealth more generally.

The period between the end of Second World War and the mid-1970s was characterised, across the world, by greater popular faith in the constructive potential of centralised governance than any era in modern history.[1] It was entirely logical that this should have been so. Centralised approaches had proved their worth in tackling the two great crises of the preceding decades: the great depression and then the Second World War. The war was, not incidentally, followed by over two decades of centralised governance in which the world economy flourished. A widespread belief in such approaches was thus to be expected – and in that era, it was apparent in both the Soviet and Western blocks, and in the new nations of Asia and Africa, many of which joined the Commonwealth.

But then during the mid-1970s and the early 1980s, a precipitate loss of confidence in centralised governance occurred – again globally. Or rather, since it had been gradually gestating for some time, it crystallised in that period. It was triggered in part by the oil shocks following the 1973 Middle East war. But the complacency, excesses and harmful policies of politicians – not least those who belonged to the first generation of leaders in newly independent countries in Commonwealth Africa and Asia – contributed mightily to it.

This loss of confidence naturally inspired a search for alternatives to centralised governance and state-led development. Initially, while Reagan and Thatcher influenced international affairs, the main alternative that people seized upon was market forces. But they eventually produced their own share of troubles – especially in less developed countries (many of them Commonwealth member states) which undertook 'structural adjustment' programmes.

Given that harsh and often unproductive experience, other alternatives to centralised governance began to appear more attractive. They included civil society, human rights, democratic decentralisation, micro-credit and bottom-up participatory approaches to development. These themes eventually became important new elements in the strategies adopted by international development agencies – and within both the official and non-official Commonwealth. But Sonny's time as Secretary-General was marked by an array of difficulties within member countries in adjusting to the loss of confidence in centralised governance, and to new uncertainties and realities. (It was not until after his period that two further trends acquired great momentum: globalisation and terrorism.)

The leaders of the four countries of Commonwealth South Asia were all confronted with these issues. But with one exception (which then went badly wrong), they refused to recognise them and to respond imaginatively. Their actions in the period before the early 1990s tended towards purblind centralisation and assertiveness – more of the same pathology that had caused popular disillusionment. For South Asia, that era was, as Jyotirinda Das Gupta aptly put it, "A Season of Caesars".[2]

 It was only after 1990 that new leaders in some of the four countries adopted different, more constructive approaches. During the Ramphal years, those four governments mainly caused serious problems – for themselves, for the people whom they governed, and for the Commonwealth. Let us consider each of them in turn.

In July 1975 – as Sonny was preparing to assume his new role as Secretary-General two months later – Indira Gandhi imposed an Emergency in India. It was advertised as an attempt to save democracy, but its real intent was to save Mrs. Gandhi whose over-centralisation of power had alienated a vast array of interests. They included many key leaders in her own Congress Party which she had been busy weakening, since she saw it not as a useful instrument through which to govern but as a threat to her own dominance. She had also begun undermining most of the formal institutions in the political system – in the interests of personal rule.

The Emergency lasted 19 months during which many abuses, largely inspired by her son, Sanjay, defaced India. For the most part in that period, Indira Gandhi was in no position to operate constructively within the Commonwealth – although she had made one positive contribution just before, when she urged Sonny to accept the post of Secretary-General.

By over-centralising power, she had actually weakened herself in certain crucial ways. By instilling fear in her subordinates, she persuaded them to tell her only things which they thought she wanted to hear. So she called an election in early 1977 on the naïve assumption – born of sycophancy – that she would sweep back to power. Sanjay Gandhi, who had concluded that no further elections need occur, had neglected to insert his minions into India's Election Commission, so the 1977 election was free and fair. A wave of revulsion against the Emergency gave a motley and hurriedly assembled opposition front a landslide victory.

The Janata Party government which resulted ruled for a little over two years. It initiated some enlightened reforms, notably in rural development.[3]   And its Foreign (in Indian parlance, 'External Affairs') Minister, the Hindu nationalist Atal Behari Vajpayee, surprised many observers with his imaginative, moderate approach to the task. But that government was plagued by the rigidity of its Prime Minister, Morarji Desai, and more seriously by factional conflict among the contradictory forces that it contained. By early 1979, infighting had reached acutely embarrassing levels and the government was widely discredited.

Later that year, it collapsed and in January 1980, Indira Gandhi swept back to power at a general election. She again radically centralised power. For six months, her son Sanjay mounted a campaign of retribution against her opponents. But in mid-1980, he was killed when his light plane crashed while he was performing aerobatics at low altitude over New Delhi.

His death left Mrs. Gandhi deeply traumatised. Most of her attention during her remaining time in power was devoted to three things. She pursued the passage of draconian legislation to arm the government with illiberal powers. She focused inordinately upon ensuring dynastic succession for her second son, Rajiv – a reluctant recruit to politics. And she indulged in the manipulation of religious sentiments on the dangerous assumption that parochialism was safe in her hands.[4]

To divide her opponents in Punjab, she encouraged the emergence of a Sikh extremist. When his popularity soared and he took up residence in the Golden Temple in Amritsar, the holiest Sikh shrine, she caused profound anger among the Sikhs by sending in the army. This led to a decade of terrorism and conflict in and beyond Punjab which compromised the defence of India, and in October 1984, to the assassination of Indira Gandhi by her Sikh bodyguards. During this period, she and her government were unable to serve as a positive force in wider Commonwealth affairs.

She was succeeded by her son Rajiv who won a landslide victory on a sympathy wave at a national election in late 1984. Many hoped that he would provide India with a fresh start. At first, during his initial two years as Prime Minister, he took several promising steps. They included a constructive role in the negotiations at the 1985 Commonwealth Heads of Government Meeting (CHOGM) over sanctions on South Africa. He and other leaders offered diverse proposals which Sonny shrewdly helped to integrate into a coherent package. Two positive outcomes ensued. First, the consensus was broad enough to persuade Margaret Thatcher, a hardened reactionary on this issue, to give a little ground – enough to make sanctions a reality. Second, the way was opened to the creation of an Eminent Persons Group which eventually helped to unpick the South African stalemate.

But Rajiv Gandhi's early promise then evaporated. When he encountered resistance to his early innovative policies, his inexperience told and he sowed confusion by reversing himself on many of the fundamental issues that he had initially tackled: economic reform,[5] the rebuilding of the Congress Party, exclusion of the coterie that had surrounded his mother, more supportive treatment of formal state institutions and alternative power centres, his approach to India's neighbours, etc. This inspired mass disillusionment within India, as groups on both sides of various issues became alienated. He was ousted from power by the electorate in 1989, after which India entered a period of great uncertainty.[6] So from the time of Rajiv Gandhi's election until Sonny Ramphal stepped down as Secretary-General in 1990, the Commonwealth had largely to make do without a coherent, constructive partner in New Delhi.

Some readers may wonder whether Pakistan should be included only as a mere footnote here, since for most of Sonny's time as Secretary-General, it was not a member of the Commonwealth. Zulfikar Ali Bhutto had withdrawn in January 1972, three years before Sonny assumed his post. Bhutto had two main, unconvincing reasons for opting out. The first was petulant to the point of silliness. He was responding to the entirely natural decisions by certain prominent member states – not least the United Kingdom – to recognise Bangladesh. It is difficult to believe that he actually expected Commonwealth governments not to do so, after Bengalis had revolted against extreme brutalities by Pakistan's army – which had, among other things, pursued a wide-ranging campaign of murder against the intelligentsia of the former East Pakistan. His second reason was similarly unpersuasive. He sought to distance Pakistan from its erstwhile friends in the West and to cultivate ties to the Middle East and, above all, China.[7] But (as someone of his sophistication surely knew) the Commonwealth was far from a tool of the West and was not associated with Pakistan's long-standing Western patron, the US. Pakistan did not rejoin the Commonwealth until 1989, when his daughter (and by then Prime Minister) Benazir attended the Kuala Lumpur CHOGM.

It is nonetheless worth considering Pakistan during the Ramphal era – and not only because in his last year, it was once again a member. A brief survey will indicate that in that period, Pakistan, like the other member-states in South Asia, was deeply troubled. Even if it had not left in 1973, it would have posed serious problems for the values of the Commonwealth.

By the time Sonny assumed his post, Mr Bhutto – a democratically elected Prime Minister – was in serious difficulties. He had governed in an authoritarian manner, over-centralising power, in ways that alienated erstwhile supporters and weakened him. Like Indira Gandhi in India, as well as Sirimavo Bandaranaike and her successors in Sri Lanka (see below), he prolonged the life of the government elected in

1970 until 1977 – in his case, by introducing a new constitution in 1973. Throughout his time in power, he maintained curbs on the press and on the operations of opposition groups. He also introduced policies during the early 1970s which angered groups (most notably the urban middle classes) that had been crucial to his 1970 election victory. He intended to compensate for this by cultivating the rural poor who had greater numerical strength. But he miscalculated badly by reaching out to them through intermediaries – the landed elite – who were plainly ill-equipped and disinclined to serve this purpose.[8]

On 7 January 1977, he called for a general election two months later – a decision that probably helped to persuade Indira Gandhi to follow suit eleven days thereafter. Like Mrs. Gandhi, he did so with great confidence that he would win, and (again like her) with too little awareness of the danger posed by the "phase of decay" that his Pakistan People's Party had undergone during his years in power. Indeed, it had "failed to convert itself into a party" at all.[9] This was the result of two tendencies which he shared with his Indian counterpart: gross over-centralisation[10] and the undermining of the autonomy and substance of key political institutions, leading to what even a sympathetic analyst described as "institutional collapse".[11] As a consequence, Bhutto – again like Indira Gandhi – "did not have the institutions that could provide him with feedback".[12] He won an apparently resounding election victory, but accusations of rigging brought opposition groups into the streets, leading to a prolonged, chaotic stalemate.[13] The army was eventually called out to deal with the agitation, and this was used in July 1977 to justify a military coup led by General Zia-ul-Haq.

Zia then constructed the most vindictive and abusive military dictatorship that Pakistan (and South Asia) has ever seen. In April 1979, Bhutto was hanged in what many observers saw as an act of judicially sanctioned murder. This inspired a wave of nausea in the international community, but after December of that year, Zia gained a relatively free hand as a result of the Soviet invasion of Afghanistan. It persuaded the U.S. to lend him strong support as a distasteful but essential ally in the struggle that then developed across Pakistan's northern border. Zia used his new found room for manoeuvre to intimidate and brutalise opponents, and he focused on themes such as the introduction of *sharia* law.

On 17 August 1988, Zia died in an air crash that may have been the result of a bomb placed on board. His murderers, if that is what they were, have never been identified. In his absence, Pakistan moved towards fresh elections in 1988, which brought Benazir Bhutto and the Pakistan People's Party back to power, although an amendment which Zia has made to the constitution still permitted his military successors to dismiss elected governments at will. The new ruling party and government, both of which Benazir ran in the centralised manner of her father, had to struggle with "an atmosphere of bigotry, fanaticism and distorted values"[14] which Zia had left behind. These things meant that when Pakistan rejoined the Commonwealth soon after, the new government was poorly placed to play a constructive role in the last year of Sonny's time as Secretary-General.[15]

Throughout nearly all of the Ramphal era, governments in both Pakistan and India tended to be inordinately and unproductively focused on the enmities that divided them and, in their internal affairs, on narrow concerns that produced no little destruction. This wrecked the first attempts to make the South Asian Association for Regional Cooperation into a viable institution. And it dashed hopes that either country might serve as a really strong and constructive force within the Commonwealth in that period.

If Indira Gandhi's Emergency had been one nasty shock for the new Commonwealth Secretary-General in 1975, the murder of the elected leader of Bangladesh, Sheikh Mujibur Rahman and most of his family in a military coup in August of that year provided another. This left Sonny – who began his new job immediately thereafter – and the Commonwealth to deal with successive military regimes in Bangladesh throughout his time in office.

The first dictator, Ziaur Rahman, grappled unsuccessfully with an insoluble problem that has always confronted juntas in Bangladesh and Pakistan: armies are inadequate instruments for governing such vast, complex societies. (This is not to suggest that they are better equipped to manage small states, but their incapacities are immensely magnified in large countries.) He was assassinated in May, 1981 by discontented elements of the armed forces. After a period of uncertainty, his immediate successors in the military were themselves toppled by fellow officers in a fresh coup ten months later. The new regime was led by General Hussein Mohammad Ershad.

Despite their coercive origins and methods, these two military governments in Bangladesh were for the most part less brutish than that of Zia-ul-Haq in Pakistan. Both sought to legitimise their rule by creating political parties which received dubious electoral mandates, and which sought to cultivate important interests by offering enticements and limited accommodations. But they were unpromising partners in Commonwealth affairs.

The Ershad government carried reform further than its predecessor by seizing upon the growing popularity of one of the alternatives to statist governance – democratic decentralisation. Ershad created a new tier of elected councils at the sub-district level, and pumped substantial resources for development into them. A key aim was to foster a set of loyal council chairmen (they were all men) at that level. This produced some minimal benefits for ordinary folk, but because the council chairmen had such unquestioning support from the apex of the regime, they grew self-indulgent and unpopular. The system was a poor substitute for genuine democracy at the national level – since governance remained, in practice, highly centralised. It ended up fuelling popular disillusionment with the regime, especially after a substantially fictitious election to decentralised bodies in 1988 which Bangladeshis rightly describe as a "voterless" election.[16]

Eventually, mass protests brought down the Ershad regime, but sadly, that did not occur until shortly after Sonny ceased to be Secretary-General. His successors were therefore able to work with governments chosen at free elections on three occasions beginning in 1992. Those governments were seriously flawed, as revelations since early 2007 have indicated, but they were distinct improvements on the old juntas. For Sonny, however, this change came too late. The Bangladeshi governments with which he had to deal were more troublesome than helpful.

Sri Lanka was, at first, the exception among the four governments of Commonwealth South Asia. Between 1970 and 1977, the government led by Mrs. Sirimavo Bandaranaike had pursued ferociously state-dominated economic policies which proved ruinous. It had also engaged in a nakedly anti-democratic manoeuvre to prolong its term in office by two years – a ploy that was described in private by a minister in her government as "just raw power".[17] At a fair election in 1977, the opposition, led by J.R. Jayewardene, swept her out of office.

He swiftly, albeit cautiously, opened the economy up to market forces – anticipating by 14 years a similar change in India. This gradually yielded some developmental gains, although not enough to avoid severe alienation among poorer people in both of the island's linguistic groups. In 1978, his government adopted a new French-style constitution. This was achieved by highly dubious means, but it had one promising feature. It was intended to make votes from the dangerously alienated Tamil minority actually count – for the first time – in the decision on the great prize in the new political system, the potent executive presidency.[18]

But the promise of the new structures was soon swallowed up by catastrophically ill-considered actions. The Jayewardene government took vengeful measures against Mrs. Bandaranaike, and then in 1982 held a rigged referendum which "approved" the prolongation – without a general election – of the term of the government elected five years earlier.[19] That episode was strongly reminiscent of the similar manoeuvre by the previous government a decade before which had done so much to discredit it.

Things degenerated much further the following year when prominent figures in the government fomented and carefully coordinated vicious anti-Tamil riots which left the minority in such despair that a full-scale civil war broke out between the security forces and the Liberation Tigers of Tamil Eelam (LTTE).[20] It persists to this day[21] and has claimed the lives of 70,000 people. It is well known that the LTTE has employed terrorist tactics, including suicide bombings which it has the dubious distinction of pioneering. But what is often forgotten is that during the 1980s, the security forces also made extensive use of state terrorism against the minority, especially massacres of unarmed Tamil non-combatants. Not one but two terrorist forces were at work. Ghastly atrocities committed by both sides fostered appallingly destructive extremism and obduracy within each.

One other, thoroughly vile enormity which occurred during the Ramphal term as Secretary-General is also often forgotten. In the late 1980s, a revolt among deprived members of the Sinhalese (majority) community was simmering mainly in Sri Lanka's Southern Province, led by the Janatha Vimukthi Peramuna. The government's intelligence gathering on the identities of the radicals was woefully inadequate, so it adopted an indiscriminate extermination campaign against mainly young people from that province. Thousands were slaughtered. Sri Lanka had become one of the worst killing fields on earth.[22]

In those excessively polite pre-Harare days, it was difficult for these terrible actions even to be raised in public discussions in Commonwealth forums. When this writer did so at a workshop, a Sri Lankan bureaucrat working for the Commonwealth Secretariat expressed astonishment at the mere mention of such unpleasant "myths." But leading figures in the Commonwealth were well aware of the ghastly reality, and of the deep enmity that divided the island's two linguistic groups.

Indeed, early in his time as Secretary-General – before a full scale civil war had broken out in Sri Lanka – Sonny had quietly and characteristically made an attempt to promote an accommodation between Sinhalese and Tamils. This might have prevented this terrible and so far (after 24 years) unwinnable conflict from happening. But, like all similar diplomatic overtures over the years, his effort ran aground amid stubbornness and spite on both sides. In the Ramphal era, Sri Lanka's government was both disinclined and unfit to make a constructive contribution to the work of the Commonwealth.

Things improved for a spell after 1994 – too late for Sonny. The newly elected President, Chandrika Kumaratunga, offered the Tamil minority the most generous and imaginative set of proposals that the island has ever seen. But extremists in both the LTTE and the Sinhalese majority thwarted her efforts to resolve the conflict, and the civil war has lately revived.

This adds up to a bleak narrative. In fairness, it should be said that many professional diplomats and technocrats worked admirably for the various regimes discussed above, and did their best to enable them to make positive contributions at home, within the Commonwealth, and in other international arenas. But there were tight limits on what they could achieve, given the character of the governments for which they toiled.

During Sonny's time as Secretary-General, all four South Asian member governments posed severe problems for the Commonwealth. If the mechanisms which have resulted from the Harare Declaration of 1991 had been available to him, he and his colleagues might have been able to encourage more enlightened international and domestic policies by governments in South Asia – although that might also have meant that countries containing a sizeable majority of the population of the Commonwealth could have been frozen out for much of the time. And given the determinedly destructive tendencies of most of the senior political leaders in those countries in that era, it is entirely possible that despite this, little progress would have been made in persuading them to govern more humanely at home and to operate more congenially at the international level.

As the contents of this book and plenty of other evidence indicate, Sonny Ramphal is properly regarded as a highly successful Commonwealth Secretary-General. But one aim of this chapter is to suggest that his achievements have actually been underestimated – because many observers do not fully recognise the difficulties that he faced. It is generally understood that he and the Commonwealth faced excruciating problems arising from southern Africa. But it is less well known that he had to deal with troubled and troublesome regimes in South Asia as well. For most of his time at the helm, they represented dead weight or worse, sometimes a great deal worse. And yet he and the Commonwealth still managed to make considerable headway on many fronts. To have accomplished so much in the teeth of the problems discussed here is quite remarkable.

— ∞ —

1   I am grateful to Geoffrey Hawthorn at the University of Cambridge for initially stressing this. I have elaborated much more fully on this theme in J. Manor, *The Political Economy of Democratic Decentralization* (The World Bank, Washington, 1998) Part II.

2   "A Season of Caesars: Emergency Regimes and Development Politics in Asia", *Asian Survey* (May 1981).

3   See for example, M.F. Franda, *India's Rural Development: An Assessment of Alternatives* (Indiana University Press, Bloomington, 1980).

4   J. Manor, "Anomie in India Politics", *Economic and Political Weekly*, Annual Number, 1983.

5   J. Manor, "Tried Then Abandoned: Economic Liberalization in India", *IDS Bulletin* (October 1987).

6   These various stories are discussed in greater detail in J. Manor, "India" in W.P. Shiveley (ed.) *Comparative Governance* (McGraw-Hill Primus, New York, 2006); and J. Manor, "Politics: Disillusionment, Ambiguity and Ferment" in M.L. Bouton (ed.), India Briefing (St. Martins Press, New York, 1988).

7   I. Talbot, *Pakistan: A Modern History* (Hurst & Co., London, 1998) pp. 234-35.

8   For a detailed account of Bhutto's years in power, see S.J. Burki, *Pakistan under Bhutto 1971-1977* (Macmillan, London, 1980). See especially, pp. 190-91.

9   A.H. Syed, "The Pakistan People's Party: Phases One and Two" in L. Ziring and W.H. Wriggins (eds.) *Pakistan: The Long View* (Duke University Press, Durham, NC, 1977) p. 115 – initially cited in ibid., p. 220.

10 Burki, *Pakistan under Bhutto...*, pp. 182-83.

11 Ibid., p.178.

12 Ibid., p.180.

13 M. Weinbaum, "The March 1977 Elections in Pakistan: Where Everyone Lost", Asian Survey (July 1977).

14 Talbot, *Pakistan: A Modern History,* p. 286.

15 For other perceptive accounts of Pakistan, see M. Lodhi, *Pakistan's Experience with Democracy* (Vanguard, Lahore, 1994) and *The External Dimension* (Vanguard, Lahore, 1994).

16 For a detailed analysis of the Ershad era and this experiment with decentralisation, see R. Crook and J. Manor, *Democracy and Decentralisation in South Asia and West Africa: Participation, Accountability and Performance* (Cambridge University Press, Cambridge, 1998) chapter three.

17 Interview with this writer, Colombo, 20 August 1978.

18 J. Manor, "A New Political Order for Sri Lanka", *The World Today* (September 1979).

19 'Priya Samarakone', "The Conduct of the Referendum" in J. Manor (ed.) *Sri Lanka in Change and Crisis* (Croom Helm, London, 1894).

20 See in this connection several of the chapters in ibid. and J. Manor, "Sri Lanka: Explaining the Disaster", *The World Today* (November 1983).

21 An uneasy ceasefire held between 2002 and 2006, but then broke down. Since the resumption of conflict in 2006, 5,000 people have been killed.

22 The state terrorism against the Tamil minority and against members of the Sinhalese majority in the Southern Province were politely edited out of many international reports such as the U.S. State Department's annual report to Congress on terrorism. But The Economist, the great Indian newspaper *The Hindu*, and the BBC World Service admirably reported on the reality.

A global citizen

— ∞ —

Ramphal and the Lomé Convention

Kaye Whiteman

—— ∞ ——

"To say that the seeds of the Lomé Convention were sown on the lawns of the Prime Minister's residence in Georgetown is perhaps hyperbole – but there is more than a grain of truth in it"

– from 'Remembering to Score: A Retrospective' by Sonny Ramphal (published on the Caribbean website www.silvertorch.com)

When Sonny Ramphal became Guyana's Foreign Minister in 1972, the timing could not have been more propitious. Wide-ranging international changes were afoot, in the Caribbean, in Europe, and in the world. In the Caribbean, after a decade of diversity after the break-up of the West Indies Federation, new moves for solidarity were being undertaken, and Guyana was a central player. In Europe, Britain had been negotiating its difficult, late-coming entry to the then European Economic Community (EEC), realising increasingly the solitude of its post-imperial situation.

British entry, and the enlargement from six to nine, including the admission for the first time of English-speaking states, would profoundly strengthen and give credibility to Europe's role on the world stage, at a time of growing international uncertainty. The Arab-Israeli war of October 1973 (sometimes known as the Yom Kippur war), and the oil supply crisis which followed was thought by many to presage a revolution in world economic relations. This was the era of the oil weapon, of the newly-found producer power, and new

—— ∞ ——

Kaye Whiteman is a journalist who has also worked for the European Commission in Brussels and has headed the Information division for the Commonwealth Secretariat.

mechanisms produced by the crisis, such as the New International Economic Order, and the North-South Dialogue.

Much of this new conceptualising, it has to be said with hindsight, proved to be a false dawn. However, with the USA stricken by both Vietnam and Watergate, who knew where the world was heading? In these circumstances, the new deal that had been promised with the rise of nationalism in what had come in the 1950s and 1960s to be known as the Third World (following the Afro-Asian summit of 1955 in Bandoeng, and the later birth of the Non-Aligned Movement) appeared to be materialising.

From 1970 onwards, Guyana's Prime Minister Forbes Burnham, one of the shrewdest minds in Caribbean politics, even if he had cut corners in his rise to power, moved to a more radical foreign policy provoked by the need to broaden his international support because of the border dispute with Venezuela that erupted soon after independence in 1966. It was thus, probably by design, that one of Ramphal's first tasks as Foreign Minister was to chair the first meeting of Foreign Ministers of the Non-Aligned Movement to take place in the western hemisphere. This was in Georgetown, in August 1972. In the words of his son-in-law Sir Ron Sanders, in the collection of Ramphal speeches[1] from the 1970s and 1980s which he has edited, it was this conference "that brought Ramphal's negotiating skills and diplomatic capabilities to the attention of the majority of world governments." It helped to put the movement on course, after a period of several years of disarray.

In historical developments, the context in which things happen is always important. This period in the 1970s probably saw the apogee of the influence of the international activity around the New International Economic Order, and the birth of the Group of 77 which was speaking in UN fora for developing countries on economic issues. It forms essential background to understanding Ramphal's role in other sectors, not just in the Caribbean, where the decisive step forward of the creation of CARICOM (the Caribbean Community and Common Market) came in August 1973. This background was crucial in the whole context of the negotiations with Europe by the African-Caribbean-Pacific states.

Ramphal became Foreign Minister in 1972, but he had been Minister of State since 1967, concurrently with holding the job of Attorney-General. He had therefore been involved in the discussions with Britain over arrangements for Commonwealth countries in the Heath government's discussions with the EEC, which eventually produced Protocol 22 of the British Accession Treaty, signed in May 1972. This treaty committed the parties to defend the transfer of Commonwealth Preference at least as far as Africa, the Caribbean and Pacific were concerned, and to "have at heart" the interests especially of the sugar producing countries of the Commonwealth (the Caribbean, plus Mauritius and Fiji). These commitments were the basis for far-reaching diplomatic developments.

In early 1973, when Britain eventually joined the EEC, there was actually an apparently confused situation. Although the relevant countries of the Commonwealth were invited to negotiate what were called in Euro-parlance 'Association agreements', they had come up against the vested interests of those in Africa that already had a comprehensive trade and aid agreement, the 18 countries of the Yaoundé Convention (14 of which were ex-French territories). These, with their allies in Europe, were keen to preserve the privileges they were already enjoying. Initially they worked against the idea of a wider agreement linking 'associates' and 'associables' under a big tent in which all of sub-Saharan Africa negotiated with Europe, alongside the Caribbean and Pacific states.

The possibility of this wider agreement had been presaged as early as October 1972 by Arnold Smith, the then Commonwealth Secretary-General in a letter[2] written to the relevant 19 Commonwealth Foreign Ministers saying that Commonwealth leaders had told him that they did not want to be fitted into a framework worked out several years before: "What they appear to be looking toward is a freely negotiated relationship between the enlarged Community and themselves, which provided for mutually beneficial trade and commodity arrangements and development assistance – but with a non-discriminatory character." This latter point, that the reciprocity provisions of the Yaoundé Convention should be dropped in any new accord was a constant theme of the coming months, to which Ramphal also lent his own imprimatur.

It had been at an outdoor reception at the Prime Minister's residence, at the same 1972 Non-Aligned Meeting in Georgetown, that Ramphal had taken several Caribbean and African ministers aside for an informal meeting to discuss the coming relations with the enlarged EEC "to see if we can get other people to pool their resources with ours in relation to the negotiations that lie ahead". This was followed by a visit by officials, including Allister McIntyre, from the then Carifta (Caribbean Free Trade Area, precursor of CARICOM) to east and west Africa, to produce a coordinated position at a series of Ministerial Meetings.

Ramphal remained closely involved with the diplomacy. After a historic declaration of support for a unified African negotiation at the OAU's Tenth Anniversary Summit in Addis Ababa in May 1973, followed up at an ad hoc Ministers Meeting in Lagos, the three groups – Africa, Caribbean and Pacific went together to Brussels at the end of July, for what the EEC had proposed as the formal opening of negotiations. These in fact took place only in October. Ramphal then made an important gesture, by requesting the African spokesman Wenike Briggs, Nigeria's Trade Commissioner, to speak on behalf of the Caribbean. This gesture was then emulated by the Pacific spokesman, Ratu Mara of Fiji. The outcome signified the initiation of a single voice for the ACP.

The preceding July meeting however, provided the opportunity for Ramphal, as spokesman for the Caribbean Group, to set out his stall in the elegant language of diplomacy, as *"a dialogue between one economic community and another"*. These were for the three groups 'talks about talks', to establish the correct bases for negotiations. Aware that there were many who were dragging their feet, he said "we interpret the statements made [by the EEC]....to mean that in its approach to the negotiations, the community is not hidebound by existing stereotypes but is willing to formulate new modes best capable of meeting current realities and reflecting contemporary ideas.... We have many reservations on the character of the model; but so long as our negotiations are conditioned not by the precedents of a passing era but by a resolve to identify a model of arrangements more relevant to the needs and mood of the 70s and beyond, there is no reason to doubt our joint capacity to devise it."

This is classic Ramphal language, revealing his role as the philosopher of the project and his strategic and intellectual input. The whole tone of the speech was intended to appeal to the EEC, to transcend its desire to stick by existing arrangements and go for something new that would be a genuinely new agreement. It should meet, as he said "the needs and mood of the 70s", of which Brussels must have been acutely aware. He stressed the importance of regional cooperation, as much a theme in Europe as in the three developing regions. Most of all, central to his speech, as with those of the other groupings, was the rejection of the idea that "the negotiations should proceed on the concept of a free trade relationship," echoing the original view of Arnold Smith quoted above, which articulated the whole philosophy of the Commonwealth Preference that was buried in Britain's Accession Treaty. In a typical Ramphal formulation of delicate but devastating irony, he said "we hesitate to believe that the community seriously seeks such entry and we can see no rational basis on which we should be required to grant it in the context of arrangements intended to promote our economic development."

It was put more directly by the Nigerian leader, General Yakubu Gowon, two weeks later at the seminal Commonwealth Heads of Government Meeting (CHOGM) in Ottawa Canada. "We must of necessity trade with Europe and the rest of the world". He said. *"But we also want the world to know that it is fiction to speak of a free trade area between developed and developing countries."* This was a constant of the negotiations, that eventually formed the basis of the Lomé Convention between the EEC and the African Caribbean and Pacific Group, signed on 28 February, 1975. It was an agreement hailed as unprecedented between North and South, and one substantially made possible by the likes of Ramphal of the ACP and Claude Cheysson, French Development Commissioner of the EEC.

Studying copies of the *EEC-ACP Courier* (formerly *Courier of the Association*), – apart from noting how slow it was to dawn in Brussels that there was such a thing as the ACP Group – one detects that Ramphal withdrew after negotiating the main framework of the new ACP-EEC trade regime. He then left his colleagues such as PJ Patterson, then Jamaica's Minister of Trade and Industry, to play a key role in negotiating the crucial Sugar Protocol. The Caribbean's accomplished representatives in Brussels, such as Frank Francis for Jamaica and O'Neill Lewis for Trinidad were also staunch players, while Edwin Carrington, the Trinidadian technocrat representing CARICOM, complemented the team. Carrington went on to be a central player in the African Caribbean and Pacific Group; with his vast knowledge of the whole EU-ACP relationship, he ended up as ACP Secretary-General. One of the successes of the Lomé negotiations was the way in which the diplomats of the different regions interacted.

Many observers of the negotiations have noted the real nexus that had been worked out between the Caribbean and African representatives, including leaders such as Wenike Briggs of Nigeria, Colonel Roger Felli of Ghana, Babacar Ba of Senegal and Robert Ouko of Kenya. Ramphal himself acknowledges that this was a vital element in putting the final convention together. And if the Sugar Protocol was negotiated separately by the Caribbean, the whole package benefited from the weight of the African presence at the negotiation.

His own speech (as Caribbean spokesman) at the signing of the convention in Lomé made much of that tripartite group unity, and if with hindsight his hope seems over-optimistic, at the time it was surely justified.

The negotiations, he said, had been "testimony to an even more ample fulfilment of the ambition for unity dimly perceived and cautiously advanced at the start of the negotiations...I venture to suggest that the reality, tested as it has been in these negotiations, is of immense importance, not merely for the strengths it brings to our group of states and therefore to the operating of the convention, but for the new dimension it contributes to the efforts of our generation to evolve the structures of an interdependent world society." Indeed, he added that the ACP remained determined to ensure that "the convention contributed to the realisation of the aspirations of the international community..." He acknowledged that it would be a "dangerous pretence" to believe that the document fulfilled all those ideals, and it was in its potential rather than its text that its true value laid.

However, it seemed normal and inevitable that the decision of the ACP to formalise its existence as a separate grouping rather than a simple offshoot of negotiations with the EEC and later the European Union, should have been made in Georgetown in June. The charter setting up the ACP Group was also named after the Guyanese capital. Ever the strategist, the key role Ramphal had played in the formation of the

ACP as a group was thus recognised.

His achievements in helping to put together the Lomé deal had also helped build him a formidable constituency among Commonwealth members in the developing world, especially in Africa. This helped to make him the obvious and ultimately unanimous candidate to succeed Arnold Smith at the Kingston Commonwealth Heads of Government Meeting in 1975, later in the same year, after Lomé and the Georgetown agreement.

As Commonwealth Secretary-General, he continued to maintain an active interest in the performance of the Lomé Convention, using the limited funds available to provide Commonwealth technical assistance when it came to renegotiating the conventions in 1979, 1984 and 1989. Each time, it has to be said, there was less negotiating muscle than the last, in part because of the economic collapse of Africa in the 1980s, but also because of the growing internal problems of the convention itself, as well as conflicts within the ACP group. In the 1990s Ramphal returned to a role in the negotiations for the successor to Lomé. After the Commission's 'Green Paper' of 1997, in which the possibility of disbanding the ACP was evoked, Ramphal produced a passionate plea, at a consultative meeting in London, which was published in the same *EU-ACP Courier* later that year under the title of "The Argument Against Splitting the ACP." It was a plea that may have worked, even if the end product in the Cotonou Agreement of June 2000 was a disappointment on the trade side because of the key decision to abandon non-reciprocity, with an eight year grace period (although one has to bear in mind that the sinews of the agreement were always in the aid package, however imperfectly it may have been implemented).

Disillusionment after Cotonou returned with reciprocity (under pressure, it seems from the newly reinforced World Trade Organisation). The ACP-EU relationship embarked on what now seems a downward path, with the ACP being parcelled into six groupings for Economic Partnership Agreements, and then in 2005 being subjected to three separate EU strategy papers. Times have changed dramatically, and the EU now has 27 member states, and a different appraisal of its own putative foreign and security policies. It now appears in Brussels as if the ACP Group has less and less power and relevance, especially as the EU now seems determined to build up a separate relationship with Africa. Although the Cotonou agreement lasts until 2020, there is a risk that the ACP Secretariat and the structures of the group will increasingly live in a kind of virtual reality.

If Ramphal may now be looking on the aftermath of his own work with disappointment, we should still return for solace to a uniquely beautifully Ramphalesque quote in his speech in Lomé in February 1975 from a Robert Browning poem, *"Ah, but a man's reach should exceed his grasp – or what's heaven for."*

Certainly, history will recall that Ramphal spearheaded the creation of arguably the most significant grouping of developing countries in the last quarter of the twentieth century. It would be for those who have virtually dismantled it to account to that same history.

1   *Inseparable Humanity: An Anthology of Reflections of Shridath Ramphal,* introduced and edited by Ron Sanders (publisher Hansib, London, 1988)
2   Arnold Smith papers, Commonwealth Secretariat Library 2004/078

Practising development cooperation: Ramphal's role and influence

Bishnodat Persaud

— ∞ —

Shridath Ramphal has played a distinguished role as a Commonwealth, international and Caribbean statesman and diplomat. His major contribution to South African liberation stands out among his immense achievements. There are other substantial political and diplomatic contributions through his promotion of international peace, security, justice, human rights and democracy. Yet it is doubtful that his political statesmanship is as substantial as his economic one. This may seem a controversial statement. This essay elucidates it by attempting to give, to the extent possible in limited space, an account of his economic engagements.

Ramphal's political interventions are discussed elsewhere in this volume. His political and diplomatic contributions are relevant to both the economic and political spheres, and the distinction between the two types is not an easy one to make. A notable example is his substantial role in the struggle to end the apartheid regime in South Africa. This seems to be a political contribution, yet it has a strong economic content. It was the Commonwealth, under Ramphal's guidance and prompting, as discussed in the essay by S K Rao, that started the process of economic sanctions that were to be so effective in forcing the pace of change in South Africa. The content of the policy had a lot to do with anticipation, technical guidance and the

— ∞ —

Professor Bishnodat Persaud was Director of the Economic Affairs Division at the Commonwealth Secretariat for 10 of the 15 years that Shridath Ramphal was Secretary-General. He served as adviser to Ramphal in the Brandt and South Commissions, and in his Chairmanship of the UN Committee for Development Planning.

lead role of the Secretariat in the evolution of a process of selective sanctions.

As Secretary-General of the Commonwealth, Ramphal played a key role in getting the Commonwealth and the Secretariat substantially involved in the North/South dialogue, early in his tenure. But beyond this Commonwealth participation, and related to it, he became personally engaged in a number of high level international and regional commissions concerned with development. He also chaired a central UN committee on the subject, the Committee on Development Planning, later renamed the Committee on Development Policy.

These appointments to international commissions were in his personal capacity, although they had the quiet blessing of the Commonwealth, which facilitated very effective participation, through support from Secretariat staff. Beyond the Secretariat's own high profile participation in the North/South dialogue, there was the regular work of the Secretariat concerned with assisting developing member countries, including its numerous small state members, through Commonwealth technical cooperation. His influence on the direction of this work and its priorities must also be gleaned to assess his mark on it. This aspect was not entirely separate from his involvement in international economic relations, as international development cooperation could not be without influence on development policy priorities in the Secretariat.

Even though Ramphal's 15 years at the Secretariat has a central place in his career, his contributions have a much wider range. They are so varied and complex that, in considering them, a useful distinction is not between Secretariat and non-Secretariat activities, but between his high profile international and regional involvement, through the Secretariat and otherwise, and his practical achievements in policy terms, both through the Secretariat, and before and after he was there.

His activity in economic discussion and negotiations must take into account: his active membership of major international economically-oriented commissions such as the Brandt, Brundtland and South commissions; the large role he engineered for the Commonwealth Secretariat in international economic discussions and negotiations;

the many expert groups on major economic issues set up by the Commonwealth during his stewardship at the Secretariat; and his chairmanship for three years of the high-level UN Committee for Development Planning, which reported directly to the Economic and Social Council

But it must take into account also, the large recognition he secured as Foreign Minister of Guyana, just before he came to the Secretariat, in helping to weld together African, Caribbean and Pacific countries to negotiate jointly for a single association agreement with the European Economic Community. This culminated in the Lomé Convention, which still exists, even though in changed form and name, and the establishment, more permanently, of the ACP Group and an ACP Secretariat.

His international activities continued after he left the Secretariat, in his appointment, soon after as Co-Chair with the Prime Minister of Sweden of the International Commission on Global Governance, a substantial concern of which was global economic governance and to the West Indian Commission, as Chairman, to help chart a future course for the Caribbean Community. Also, in 1997, he was offered by Caribbean Heads of Government a very practical role in international negotiations, when he was appointed as chief negotiator for the region in its international trade negotiations. He proceeded to set up, in this role, the Caribbean Regional Negotiating Machinery, which is now well established and is making a huge difference to the region's international trade negotiating capacity and expertise.

It is worth turning to some specific contributions. The most notable international commissions on which he served were the Brandt Commission on Development, and the Brundtland Commission on Environment and Development. In these, as well as in the South Commission, he played a prominent role. This resulted not only from his eminence as a thinker, statesman and diplomat, but also from his natural activism. He strongly believed – and taught many of us who worked closely with him in supporting roles – that if you wish to influence a report, you must work harder than others, and help with the drafting.

On the Brandt Commission, apart from the late Willy Brandt, the former German Chancellor, who was chairman, the two most prominent commissioners were the late Ted Heath, the former UK Prime Minister, and Ramphal himself. The report of the Brandt Commission, 'North-South: A Programme for Survival' was published in 1980. It had a tremendous reception. But the finalising of that report illustrates very well the tendency of Sir Shridath to emerge in a central role in these commissions.

What is probably not known outside the narrow circle of the commission's operation and received no public airing, was the difficulty faced by the commission in concluding a consensus report. The commission was divided between those who wanted to hold rigidly to a radical programme of change in areas such as commodities and finance to create a New International Economic Order and others, who had a more liberal stance and were conscious of the need to have a programme of recommendations that would help to break the stalemate that had developed in progress towards comprehensive North/South negotiations. The division was not helped by the fact that it was mirrored in the commission's own secretariat, no doubt encouraged by senior staff seeking alignments and mutual support with particular members.

Willy Brandt as chairman took firm action to break this deadlock between factions. He got agreement that a committee of three members, Ramphal, Ted Heath and himself, would work on a compromise draft and this operation would be shifted from the dissensions in the Brandt secretariat's base in Geneva to the Commonwealth Secretariat in London. Difficult chapters were then redrafted and pre-negotiated by assistants of the three members and then resolved at weekly meetings among Ted Heath, Ramphal and a representative of Willy Brandt. The stalemate was thus broken and a final report was agreed by the commission at a meeting in the amenable, elegant and art-rich atmosphere of Leeds Castle, in Kent in England.

The difficult economic conditions of the time, made publication of the Brandt Report timely. Its high quality and the eminence of its members, who were active in its follow-up, ensured excellent public interest. Perhaps no other international development report had such salience, when it was launched. At its first public release in The Hague, over

4,000 people turned up at a huge conference hall to welcome it. In London, a mass lobby of parliament by some 10,000 supporters of the report actually induced a more favourable governmental attitude. It was discussed in several parliaments, including the UK's and the European Parliament. Unfortunately it did not have a similar impact in the US.

This report was made available in 20 languages. A favourable outcome was the support which arose for its overarching recommendation, for a representative World Summit to take forward its proposals. This was held in Cancun in Mexico in 1981 with the sponsorship of President Portillo of Mexico and Chancellor Kreisky of Austria, who had the active support of Prime Minister Trudeau of Canada. But not all the major countries gave enthusiastic support, and the impetus began to wane.

The commission's members were not deterred, and the critical situation continuing to face developing countries encouraged them to produce a second report. Their general feeling of urgency, accentuated by the problem of debt, is reflected in the name of the second report. The 'Common Crisis' came out in 1982 and was produced in London on a similar basis to the final stages of the first report. Once again the lead role was played by Ramphal, Heath and Brandt, except that the whole report was now drafted in the Commonwealth Secretariat in London, with the Brandt Commission's only senior staff member in London, Robert Cassen, acting as drafting coordinator. He was greatly assisted by the staff of the Secretariat. This, and the location of the work in the Secretariat, gave Ramphal much control and influence.

The attempt to maintain the interest engendered by the first report met a changing international environment. The developing countries were continuing to have a difficult time as were the developed countries, which inhibited their response. All non-oil producing countries were severely affected by the second oil shock in the early 1980s. Also, the push for market-based economics and privatisation in domestic economies, especially by the Thatcher and Reagan administrations, spilled over to international policies and had a baleful influence on multilateral approaches, which, however, still greatly needed further support to enhance progress in development cooperation.

Increased financial assistance to the developing world was not forthcoming, even though it was not precluded by the new emphasis on markets. It was still needed, in ways that would enable developing countries, especially the poorer ones, to make better use of market opportunities. In the 1980s in fact, the North/South dialogue and the pressure by developing countries for comprehensive international negotiations, lost its momentum. In this situation, the developing countries took the initiative to set up their own Commission – the South Commission – in 1987. Ramphal's involvement in this, both in its formation and his membership, is taken up later.

The World Commission on Environment and Development was set up in 1983 under the chairmanship of the Prime Minister of Norway, Gro Harlem Brundtland. Mrs Brundtland insisted on Ramphal's membership. This had come to mean by now that there would also be back-up by the internationally attuned expertise in the Commonwealth Secretariat – particularly its Economic Affairs Division. Although established to operate on an independent basis, the Brundtland Commission had UN sponsorship. Its report, 'Our Common Future,' was presented to the UN in 1987.

This report too had a tremendous impact. It was a major contributor to the revival of international concerns about the environment, which had gone into retreat after the first major international conference on the subject in 1972 – the UN Conference in Stockholm on the Human Habitat. The Brundtland Report was the first to deal with environment and development in an integrated way, by developing the holistic concept of sustainable development. This expression rose into popular usage, because it was easily understood, and because of its value as a conceptual tool.

The influential membership of the commission, the depth and comprehensiveness of its report and the emphasis given to poverty, equitable development and long-term considerations, gave the report its great salience. A particular success of the commission was to encourage the developing countries to become engaged in environmental issues. There was at that time much suspicion in the developing world that the developed world was forcing environment onto the international agenda, in its own interest, and in order to downplay development. In giving emphasis to poverty and its alleviation as a priority for sustainable development, the commission greatly helped to remove this suspicion and to place sustainable development centre stage. Ramphal was a leading proponent of the poverty /environment dimension.

The report created much of the momentum which then developed for the Earth Summit in 1992, in Rio de Janeiro. As a result of his recognised contribution to the commission's work and the Commonwealth's own timely Expert Group Report on Climate Change which came out in 1989, reflecting his deep interest in the environment, he became a leading spokesman on the subject. He was appointed in 1990, when he was leaving the Commonwealth Secretariat, President of the World Conservation Union (IUCN), the powerful international governmental, non-governmental and science network on nature conservation. He served in this non-executive capacity until 1993. For the Earth Summit, he was asked by its Secretary-General, Maurice Strong, to write the official background document for the summit – the counterpart to Barbara Ward's 'Only One Earth' written for the Stockholm conference. Ramphal called it 'Our Country, The Planet.' It was published as a book in several languages and widely circulated.

The idea of a South Commission emerged at a meeting in 1986 of leading development professionals from the South, sponsored by the Third World Foundation, and hosted by Malaysia. The Prime Minister of Malaysia, Dr Mahathir bin Mohamad was given, with Ramphal who was also present, the lead role in organising the establishment of the commission. The Malaysian Prime Minister sought and got official endorsement of the idea at the Non-Aligned Summit in Harare later that year.

It was decided that if financial support was forthcoming, and establishment was feasible, Julius Nyerere, the former President of Tanzania, would be asked to chair the commission. Ramphal played a lead role in fund-raising and was given the task to design the structure and functioning of the commission and its secretariat. The Prime Minister of Malaysia, Julius Nyerere and Ramphal agreed the membership and Manmohan Singh of India, later to become Prime Minister of India, was appointed member and a full-time Secretary-General. The commission was established in 1987

The South Commission's report, 'The Challenge to the South,' was published in 1990. Again, a consensus on focus and direction was not easy to obtain. Ramphal, in the formative stage, saw the work as a great opportunity to provide guidance, not only to secure better strategy and solidarity in dealing with the North and to improve South-South cooperation, but also to ensure more forceful economic reform in the South. Manmohan Singh shared Ramphal's enthusiasm for this forward-looking and self-reliant stance. It was this approach to domestic economic reform that was to make him later, as Finance Minister and Prime Minister of India, the architect of a very successful Indian economic strategy. Sadly, this ambition for the report got diluted.

The balance in the report did not tilt enough this way. A report that could have been in the forefront of reform in the South, which came anyway belatedly in the 1990s, missed its opportunity. There was an expectation that Chairman Nyerere, who had not long before accepted the failure of his economic policies in Tanzania as its long-time President, would have been more open to reform, and would have wanted to use the commission to do much exploration of the reform process.

In this commission, however, the chairman proved a reluctant reformer, and joined with the others there who were not reform-minded. This inhibited the secretary-general, who was disinclined to challenge the chairman intellectually. The opportunity was thus lost for pioneering a new domestic policy thrust for the developing countries, for which the policy environment was becoming more amenable. Ramphal and his western hemisphere colleagues in the Commission, Michael Manley, the former Prime Minister of Jamaica and Carlos Andres Perez, the former President of Venezuela, worked together with a few others. They favoured a larger attention to domestic Southern policy reform, but they did not have much success.

An attempt at the drafting stage, by the three from the western hemisphere, to float an alternative draft introductory chapter – which would have set the stage for the report – met with much hostility from Nyerere as chairman. This led to some tension throughout the work and influenced the follow-up activities after the report was produced; a key follow-up was the setting up of a South Centre in Geneva. In the absence of a South Secretariat, this was a significant outcome. But its work, dominated by the more radical approaches, has had little influence on international economic relations or development policy. Developments in the 1990s proved that the Ramphal stance could have had greater possibilities, and it could have led to more influential institution-building in support of the South through a South Secretariat, the need for which always had Ramphal's enthusiastic support.

A further international commission on which he sat before he left the Commonwealth Secretariat was the Commission on Disarmament and Security. Although not an economic commission, it had some bearing on development cooperation. The Chairman was Olof Palme, the former Swedish Prime Minister. The Report, 'Common Security' published in 1982, helped to bring to the fore the large expenditure on armaments, and the debilitating effect this was having on development. There was a large diversion of resources in developing countries themselves, and the cost of arms became a resource constraint for developed countries, in limiting their willingness to assist with development finance.

Ramphal's appointment as Chairman of the UN Committee on Development Planning, which had hitherto been a purely economic expert body, was an attempt by the UN Secretary-General to breathe life into its work. Ramphal then encouraged the appointment of Robert McNamara for the same reason. The arrival of these men helped to give more salience to the work of the committee; it was already known for its excellent reports, but they did not have the impact they deserved.

In the 1990s, although Ramphal had now left the big stage of the Commonwealth Secretariat, his international reputation ensured a continuing high-level involvement. Immediately on leaving the Secretariat, he returned to service in the Caribbean as Chairman of the West Indian Commission, an eminent group of Caribbean personalities appointed by Caribbean Community Heads of Government to chart the community's future. The commission's influential report, 'Time for Action,' was published in 1992. It remains a guiding document for the Caribbean Community's evolution and a work of frequent reference. A recommendation for major institutional change – the establishment of a Caribbean Commission – to ensure more effective regional leadership, and quick implementation of decisions, is now being revived and is under active consideration.

Internationally Ramphal served as a member of the Carnegie Commission on preventing deadly conflict, and as Co-Chair with Ingvar Carlsson, Prime Minister of Sweden, of the International Commission on Global Governance. The latter, which also looked at how to improve the international economic architecture at the start of the 21st century, was significantly concerned with international economic relations.

Ramphal has had time also for specific projects of an economic and political nature. This allowed him to resume practical contributions, especially for the Caribbean. Mention is already made of his appointment as chief negotiator for the Caribbean in external trade policy and Head of the Caribbean Regional Negotiating Machinery. These practical engagements give some balance to his by now large bundle of international cerebral, pressure group, lobbying and negotiating type activities.

One of Ramphal's most distinctive contributions in Commonwealth history has been the creative way he set up and used Commonwealth Expert Groups. The 1975 Commonwealth Heads of Government Meeting in Kingston, Jamaica, which chose him as Secretary-General also set up, according to its communiqué, an expert group to "draw up a comprehensive programme of practical measures designed to promote development and increase the transfer of real resources to developing countries, directed at closing the gap between the rich and the poor countries." The eminent Caribbean economist, Allister McIntyre, the then Secretary-General of CARICOM, was appointed its chairman.

The background in 1975 was an enhanced dialogue on development issues between developed and developing countries, which had commenced after OPEC had steeply increased the price of oil in the early 1970s. Commonwealth involvement in the dialogue was encouraged also by the Commonwealth Singapore Declaration of 1971, which called for progressive removal of the wide disparities of wealth in the world. A unanimous conclusion of the Heads of Government Meeting in Kingston was that there was "a need for immediate steps towards the creation of a rational and equitable new international economic order." In the context of the subsequent demise of the North/South dialogue just over a decade later, this, with hindsight, was indeed a very bold mandate for Commonwealth involvement in global economic issues.

The McIntyre group was followed by twelve further economic expert groups, during Ramphal's tenure as Secretary-General. Nearly all focused on important global issues. He himself enhanced this new direction in Commonwealth work. New policy directions in the Commonwealth are set or initiated by Commonwealth governments. But very often initiatives result from approval for proposals which have been put forward by the Secretary-General, or senior management. Where proposals by the Secretariat are likely to be controversial, the prior lobbying of sympathetic governments to ensure support is a usual practice, as it is in other international organisations.

What I have not mentioned so far is Ramphal's brilliance as a diplomat. He developed such methods of prior consultation into a fine art. He had a strong interest in the Commonwealth playing a leading global role, and he used all his diplomatic skills to ensure that it did. He is a lawyer by training and this was his early profession, but as Foreign Minister in Guyana, and host to Foreign Ministers of the Non-Aligned Movement in Guyana not long before he came to the Secretariat, he had experience enough to appreciate the importance of international economics and international economic relations.

The Kingston CHOGM moved the Commonwealth in this direction, and he took it from there. He was assisted by a large economic staff, which existed then in the Secretariat. This staff was concerned with traditional and fading Commonwealth economic relations, such as commodities intelligence reports and Commonwealth preferential trade and sterling arrangements. Resources were therefore available which could be diverted to the new priorities, especially since some of the traditional concerns were ripe for review and redirection.

On arrival in Marlborough House he found two large economic divisions, which he quickly streamlined into one. The new work was more professionally demanding, but he was able to meet this challenge, because he brought in reputable economists and related professionals.

Did Ramphal have any influence on the new directions in economics that Kingston allowed the Commonwealth, even before he arrived as Secretary-General? This is an interesting question. Harold Wilson the then Prime Minister of the UK, pressed for an initiative on the commodity issue, but it was Forbes Burnham, then Prime Minister of

Ramphal's home country, Guyana, who widened the discussion to argue for action on the whole international economic order, and Ramphal was a prominent member of the Guyana delegation.

In relation to the major role of expert group reports on international issues during his tenure, it was perhaps a foretaste of things to come that his first task as Commonwealth Secretary-General was to travel through Canada on his way to take up his duties in London, to inaugurate the McIntyre group's work.

All the main subjects included in the North/South Dialogue were covered by the Commonwealth Expert Groups. Protectionism in trade policy, the Bretton Woods institutions in finance, commodities, debt, structural adjustment, gender, industrialisation, technology, climate change and the dialogue itself were all dealt with, and usually when they were prominent in wider international discussions. In fact, in the case of finance and commodities, Commonwealth interventions took place when divisions were sharp at the international level. The choice of topics for an expert group did not always reflect a response to developing country interests. It was Harold Wilson of the UK who first wanted work done on commodities, and Robert Muldoon, of New Zealand, who was keen on Bretton Woods reform. Ramphal was quick to see the possibilities such initiatives offered.

Some of the topics covered were of international interest, but were not then central to international discussion. Jobs for young people, technology, gender, the security and economic problems of small states and industrialisation were in this category and, at that time, climate change also. In these cases, there was a strong direct Commonwealth interest in the topic. Part of the objective for the expert groups was to provide guidance for policies at the Commonwealth level, and nationally. In the case of climate change, the large number of Commonwealth states vulnerable to sea level rise, such as the Maldives, was a motivating factor. The Commonwealth expert group report, which came out in 1989, was ahead of UN Intergovernmental Panel on the subject. It was the first major international report that drew attention to the seriousness of the problem.

The reports on technology, gender, debt, industrialisation and small states, all had considerable influence on subsequent Secretariat programmes. In the case of industrialisation, it led to the establishment of an Industrial Development Unit to carry out a programme of technical support in this area. The group on small states, set up in response to the Grenada invasion, brought to the fore the issues of their security and economic vulnerability. It energised a whole programme of work on small states, giving the Commonwealth a recognised central role in this area globally. In the post-Ramphal years it led to close collaboration with the World Bank, through joint Commonwealth and World Bank task forces and regular Ministerial meetings with a similar joint sponsorship.

In the case of debt, there was considerable Commonwealth fall-out from the report of an expert group chaired by Britain's Harold Lever. The group was established as a result of the international crisis arising from the huge indebtedness to international banks, of middle-income countries. But it then drew attention to the imminent problem of the official indebtedness of poor countries.

The Lever report prompted a Commonwealth initiative in the mid-1980s to address this problem by Nigel Lawson, the then UK Chancellor of the Exchequer, in collaboration with Commonwealth Finance Ministers. It led to the Commonwealth's Port-of Spain initiative from the Commonwealth Finance Ministers' meeting in that capital, and later to the international Toronto/Berlin initiatives. This sustained Commonwealth attention culminated eventually in major international action on behalf of the Highly Indebted Low Income Countries (HIPC). It was also instrumental in the Commonwealth Fund for Technical Cooperation (CFTC) promoting a computer-based debt recording and management system, which is now widely used in the Commonwealth, as well as technical assistance to member countries in debt management.

The international contribution of the expert groups and their reports was, however, circumscribed by the fact that the North-South dialogue failed to achieve much in practical terms, and had faded out by 1990. The end of the cold war put an end to the East-West competition for influence in the developing world. Thinking on development had changed among donors, and in the World Bank. There was more emphasis on market-based systems and the private sector, and the downplaying of development assistance conveniently led to its concentration on poverty reduction and a focus by the end of the century on establishing Millennium Development Goals (MDGs).

The MDGs were concerned with progress in meeting targets arising from poverty indicators. Yet this was an unbalanced focus, which neglected the need for continuing institution-building to meet even these new perspectives in development cooperation. This environment has not been conducive to comprehensive and inter-related approaches that were the essence of the North/South dialogue.

It might be thought, therefore, that a lot of the hectic Commonwealth activity in this area amounted to wasted effort. This is, however, a very superficial view. Negotiations and discussions do take place on an on-going basis periodically in specific sectors in institutions like the World Bank, the IMF, the GATT (now the WTO) and sometimes more widely in organisations like UNCTAD and the UN at its special sessions on development. The Commonwealth's work had some influence on these sectoral efforts. Sometimes it made a direct input and sometimes it was carried forward by the Secretary-General himself through his wider global engagements. It was common for meetings of Commonwealth Ministers or officials to be arranged at the venue of international negotiations. The Commonwealth's technical work developed a high reputation and it became not unusual, for instance, for the Secretary-General and his senior economic officials to give evidence to parliamentary committees and to make presentations to high level conferences on development issues.

While the dialogue did not lead to comprehensive negotiations on development cooperation, after the disappointment at Cancún, sectoral talks and approaches continued. The Commonwealth, the Brandt Commission, the South Commission, the development NGOs and other participants have all had their influence on the evolution of thinking and policies. Precise influence is a subject for clarification by scholars. More direct impacts were seen in the case of the common fund for commodities, international indebtedness, international trade policy and protectionism, climate change and the special problems of small states.

The report of the Expert Group on the Common Fund, which was chaired by Lord Campbell of Eskan, came out in 1977, at a time when there was a stalemate in UNCTAD in the negotiations. There were wide differences on the nature of the proposed fund. The Campbell group gave the options detailed consideration, and suggested ways of accommodating the positions of the main country groups. It was commended by the Commonwealth to the UN negotiating conference on the fund and became part of the official documentation.

This UN conference nevertheless broke down. Subsequently, Commonwealth Ministers concerned with commodity policy met to consider the report with a view to helping to facilitate international agreement. This meeting was able to assist convergence on the difficult issues and facilitated a resumption of the UN negotiations, which led to an agreement in 1978 and the eventual establishment of the fund. More recently, the problems which were behind the commodity issue – fluctuating prices and their secular decline – have eased because of steeply rising demand, and constrained supply. This issue is presently not regarded as a significant one.

On the Bretton Woods system, the report led to sustained Commonwealth pressure for reform through its follow-up and in the establishment by the Commonwealth of a representative consultative group. This consultative group undertook a series of interactions with the key policy-setting committees of the IMF and World Bank.

In the case of debt, the great contribution made by the Commonwealth was to highlight the issue for poor countries and set in train international action; and, has already been mentioned, it led to a great expansion in the Secretariat's own work on debt management.

On technological change, that expert group report led to institutional development in the Commonwealth by the establishment of the Commonwealth Consultative Group on Technology Management. This later led to the spawning by the Commonwealth of the Commonwealth Partnership for Technology Management, an independent institution with membership of Commonwealth and non-Commonwealth governments, business corporations and individuals active in the area of technological change.

The expert group report on climate change preceded the first report of the UN International Panel on Climate Change and was an important input into the work of the panel. This report, with its description of the risks for low-lying small states, also helped to expand the Secretariat's programme of support for them. As a result the Secretariat emerged as a leading centre in the world on research on small states issues, and for projecting their interests.

For Ramphal himself, involvement with the Commonwealth expert groups and the international commissions had other advantages. As he himself described it, it afforded him a unique opportunity to facilitate a two-way flow of information and perceptions, assisting a process of interaction to the benefit of both sets of activities.

Another positive aspect of the expert groups, not sufficiently recognised, is the association it facilitated with the many eminent personalities, that constituted their membership. This often led to a continuing cooperation and networking after their reports had appeared, and helped to promote the raised profile the Secretariat had in the Ramphal years. What may seem especially strange in today's world, is that these experts were all willing to serve the Commonwealth without payment of a fee.

The eminence of the groups and their work can be gauged from some of those involved – Lord Lever, Lord Campbell, Sir Donald Maitland, Sir Alex Cairncross, Sir Jeremy Morse, Sir Anthony Parsons and Professor Frances Stewart from the UK; Dr Manmohan Singh, Professor Tommy Koh, Dr Lal Jayawardena, Professor M.G.K Menon, Dr Arjun Sengupta, Ambassador N.Krishnan and L.K Jha from Asia; Professor H.W Arndt, Professor Stuart Harris, Professor Brownlie and Professor Snape from Australia and New Zealand; Professor Gerald Helleiner and Professor Elizabeth Mann Borgese from Canada; Sir Allister McIntyre, Willian Demas, Arthur Brown, Justice Telford Georges and Frank Rampersad from the Caribbean and Bernard Chidzero, Professor H. Onitiri, Professor J. Rweyemamu, Ambassador Olara Otunnu and Dr Dharam Ghai from Africa.

The reputation of the groups, the ideas which flowed from them and the contacts their membership provided, had a positive impact on the image and reputation of the Secretariat. This impact was not sufficiently appreciated, especially in the immediate post-Ramphal years, when the use of expert groups to enhance technical support was downplayed. There has been a reversal of this position in recent times.

Even nearing his 80th birthday, it is too early to think of Shridath Ramphal's contributions in legacy terms. He continues to be a prolific contributor. Thinking of his overall contribution today, statesmanship and diplomacy come uppermost to mind. It is hoped that this essay adds an important dimension, in showing the large content of development cooperation in that statesmanship and diplomacy. He played on the world stage, through the Commonwealth and otherwise, but he also led an energised and innovative Secretariat, in constant renewal through his fertile imagination and a heightened belief in a knowledge Secretariat, rather than mainly a bureaucratic one.

But have his economic contributions been overshadowed by his spectacular political and diplomatic achievements, as in the case of southern Africa? While it may appear so in any superficial view, this active economic involvement kept the Secretariat very much in international play, reinforcing its rationale and helping to maintain its viability. With hindsight, this would seem to be confirmed, since the demise of a large involvement in international economic relations, since Ramphal's departure as Secretary-General, has coincided with a decline in the Commonwealth's international significance.

It is possible to argue that the loss of this prominence is perhaps due to the resolution of major Commonwealth issues such as South Africa. But to say this, is not to understand the essence of Ramphal. In the context of the state of developing countries and the continuation of serious problems of poverty, human rights and civil strife in the Commonwealth and beyond, and the emergence of new ones such as security, he would have ensured a continuing substantial role for the Secretariat in international initiatives in these areas.

With Ramphal at the helm, for example, would not a Blair economic initiative and Commission on Africa have had a larger Commonwealth involvement or influence? Ramphal marched the Secretariat to the top of the hill and would have kept it there. There is much unfinished business and potential.

His administration was never a safety-first type. He was a venturesome and activist Secretary-General, as any Commonwealth Secretary-General, who is successful has to be. There is no permanence to the Commonwealth rationale and mandate, so the Commonwealth must survive by constant renewal. He allowed his senior managers full scope on routine and day-to-day matters, while he concentrated on priorities, leading edge programmes and innovations. He placed much store on advice from experts and senior managers. But he brought to bear on such advice much cogitation of his own, and an excellent judgement.

The Secretariat's technical cooperation programmes managed by CFTC, saw considerable expansion during his tenure. He gave considerable attention to its priorities. One economic area, to which he gave great attention and which was a large success for the Secretariat and CFTC, was the Technical Assistance Group, which assisted developing member countries in their negotiations with multinational corporations in areas such as mining.

In the 1980s, when interest in a North/South dialogue was waning, there was no decline in the Secretariat's activities and significance. Topics for expert groups were possibly not as major as the earlier ones, but activities continued in other areas at a hectic pace. Outside economics, there were major initiatives such as in southern Africa, general election processes and education. In the last, a major development was the establishment of the Commonwealth of Learning.

In economic affairs, Commonwealth cooperation expanded in such areas as capital markets development, foreign investment and privatisation. The Secretariat was early in pressing developing countries to be more welcoming to foreign investment, and in encouraging greater reliance on the private sector. It used its more nimble and less bureaucratic procedures to be ahead of bigger, but less flexible and more politicised international organisations on reform issues. In 1987, for instance, it produced a major publication on reform of foreign investment policy entitled 'Developing with Foreign Investment.'

The Secretariat forged ahead in facilitating capital flows to those states, not in a favourable position to attract such flows, by encouraging the setting up of private funds. A Commonwealth Equity Fund began in 1989 and plans were advanced for moving into venture capital funds. This led to the establishment of venture funds in Africa, the South Pacific and the Caribbean after Ramphal had left the Secretariat.

These activities pre-empted criticism that the Secretariat had perhaps become too global in its economic concerns, arising from the more private sector oriented and less interventionist approaches of the Thatcher government in the UK, and of other developed member countries. With strategic guidance from Ramphal and professional competence, the Secretariat was able to adjust well to the emerging situation. The Secretary-General himself was learning from the evolution of development thinking and experience.

His management style was the essence of his success. He lived dangerously, but he ensured survival, by always keeping some influential Commonwealth leaders on his side. His diplomatic approach kept powerful forces at bay among some members that got concerned that, by the 1980s, the Secretariat had too aggressive a stance on behalf of its developing country members and on issues such as South Africa. It was not surprising therefore that soon after he left, the Secretariat became bogged down with organisational and structural issues and had to endure a sizeable staff reduction and much streamlining of its activities.

Like anyone in his position, he had his critics. As someone who speaks out regularly when he sees injustices in the international system and with his continuing concern about grave inequality, he would inevitably have powerful detractors. But criticisms from high places have not deterred him, and his steadfastness has facilitated spectacular successes.

On the ideological front, it could be argued he took too interventionist a position in international economic relations. But even though not an economist, he was persuaded gradually, by his professional advisers and his experience, of the value of market-based systems and competition for efficiency and growth. He was thus able to be more on the liberal and reformist side later in his career. He exercised influence on the Brandt and South Commissions along these lines.

It is possible that his past success in bringing the African, Caribbean and Pacific countries together in their association arrangement with Europe, have encouraged him to continue to support this arrangement, which may now need rethinking in the light of changing world circumstances. But only time will tell.

In the Secretariat, his focus on change and renewal would have made some divisions and programmes, that were not in the forefront, feel neglected. But this may just have been an unavoidable issue related to priorities, delegation and the expenditure of scarce high-level management time.

Behind it all was a brilliant mind and an amiable personality. He was large in stature and in no sense a small man. He got the best from his staff and paid attention to their advancement. He was responsible for much capacity-building in institutions which he led, such as the foreign service in Guyana, the Commonwealth Secretariat and the Caribbean Regional Negotiating Machinery. One of his great legacies is the large number of people, whose self-development and motivation he greatly inspired, and through whom his spirit and work will continue, even after he ceases to be active, which hopefully is a long way off.

Bishnodat Persaud, *The Significance of Establishing a Commonwealth Equity Fund*, The Round Table, 1989

Brandt Commission, *North-South: a Programme for Survival,* MIT Press, 1980

Brandt Commission, Common Crisis: North-South Cooperation for World Recovery, Pan Books, London and Sydney, 1983

Commonwealth Secretariat, *International Economic Issues: Contributions by the Commonwealth Secretariat 1975-1990,* London 1990.

Shridath Ramphal, *Our Country, the Planet,* Island Press, Washington, 1992

South Commission, *Challenge to the South,* OUP, Oxford, 1990

West Indian Commission, *Time for Action,* Black Rock, Barbados 1992

World Commission on Environment and Development, *Our Common Future,* OUP, Oxford, 1987

Vince Cable and Bishnodat Persaud (eds), *Developing with Foreign Investment,* Croom Helm, London 1987

Ramphal's work in bridging environment and development

Vincent Cable

— ∞ —

The concept of "sustainable development", as we now use it, originated in the mid 1980s, as did the modern political debate around climate change. Sonny Ramphal played a key role in promoting both of these crucial new directions.

He had been centrally involved in the work of the Brandt Commission and the Palme Commission, both of which set out an intellectual and moral framework for looking at issues of global interconnectedness, the former in relation to trade and development and the latter on security. His particular importance was in centring discussion on the North-South dimension from the vantage point of an organisation, the Commonwealth, which had, and has, a unique mix of developed and developing countries, large and small.

It was a reflection of his political standing that when the UN Secretary General established a third global commission – this time on the environment and development – he would be asked to participate, the only individual to have the distinction of serving on all three bodies. Gro Harlem Brundtland – then Prime Minister of Norway – was asked to chair the group. This maintained a Nordic tradition which was continued in the, later, fourth commission, on Global Governance led by Sweden's Ingvar Carlsson (with Sonny Ramphal as co-Chair).

In the mid-1980s there was not the degree of environmental

— ∞ —

Vincent Cable, Deputy Leader of the Liberal Democrats in the United Kingdom, was Special Adviser on Economic Affairs to the Commonwealth Secretariat from 1983-1990, and subsequently Chief Economist at Shell.

awareness which we have today. The current anxiety about global environmental threats was somewhat remote from most political discourse. Nonetheless, understanding of ecology, the chain of reactions and dependencies which links the natural world, had been growing slowly. Television films on nature had brought into millions of homes an awareness of the diversity and richness of life as well as its fragility. Pictures of earth from space had helped to build up a sense of the planet as a whole, and its vulnerability. Rachel Carson's Silent Spring, as much as any other book, had alerted a generation to environmental side effects of chemicals. Nuclear power accidents at Three Mile Island and Chernobyl had pointed up the risks of technologies hitherto assumed to be a source of infinite supply of cheap energy.

In developing countries, the twin phenomena of deforestation and desertification had highlighted the dependence of agricultural economies on depleting environmental resources. The interconnection between development and the environment had been highlighted by Barbara Ward among others. In the UK, the International Institute for Environment and Development, particularly under the influence of the late Richard Sandbrook – also a founder of Friends of the Earth – provided intellectual stiffening. The growing salience of the issue had led to the UN's 1972 Conference in Stockholm, which led to the establishment of the United Nations Environment Programme in Nairobi later that year.

What was needed in the 1980s was a framework of analysis which brought these different strands together and, in particular, the economic and environmental components. Some divisive debates had broken out. The Club of Rome analysis had centred on limits to growth, and, in particular, the finite supply of raw materials.

While this idea was superficially plausible in the 1970s and early 80s in the wake of the two oil shocks, the arguments did not stand up to a great deal of scrutiny. Many raw materials were (and are) superabundant in relation to any likely level of demand; and the supply of recoverable reserves – oil, for example – is not fixed by nature, but interacts with prices and also with technological innovation. The two oil shock hikes, in fact, were followed by a reverse shock of two decades of depressed prices.

The "limits to growth" version of environmentalism, at least in its initial unsophisticated form, also had unfortunate normative implications. It implied that while rich countries could achieve comfortable living standards, poor countries could not expect to aspire to the same because of "limits to resources." There was certainly an element in some environmental thinking in the West which saw poor countries – with their rising populations and appetite for material improvement – as a threat.

One of Ramphal's contributions was to understand these different approaches and to find a way of reconciling them. The Brundtland Commission was the main vehicle for doing so. Like the earlier, comparable, Brandt and Palme Commissions it brought together an eclectic mix of politicians, intellectuals, journalists and public servants from a judiciously balanced collection of countries: developed, developing and communist.

All members were there in their own right rather than as government representatives (at least in theory). They varied enormously in ability, commitment, communications skills and command of English. In this group, Maurice Strong, who had chaired the Stockholm Conference was a major respected figure; Bill Ruckelshaus was a Reagan Republican, who had earlier run the Environmental Protection Agency for President Nixon, he was an important figure but somewhat detached from the political centre of gravity of the group; Emil Salim, an Indonesian minister, represented, rather effectively, the increasingly assertive, rapidly developing South East Asians; Bernard Chidzero was a major figure in the UN, later a Finance Minister in Zimbabwe.

It soon became clear that the quietly spoken Norwegian Prime Minister had a firm grip of proceedings and her simple, homely, style of speaking masked a politically sophisticated brain. She saw Sonny Ramphal virtually as co-Chair and tried throughout to reach agreement with him, as the basis for a wider consensus.

In a group of this kind there were bound to be some irreconcilable differences: between devout Latin American Catholics and Northern European ecological pessimists over population growth; between free market North American capitalists and orthodox Communists from Eastern Europe. Getting beyond sterile UN-speak and bland communiqué language was a major challenge and depended enormously on the political skills of the key members and the abilities of the Secretariat. The Commission got off to a bad start with a Canadian Secretary General who had a somewhat narrow and inflexible brand of environmentalism and only passing interest in development issues. Largely at Ramphal's prompting he was replaced by an exceptionally able Indian economist called Nitin Desai, who managed the project to a successful conclusion.

The first task of the commission was to agree on a common theme. It became "sustainable development." Much blood was spilt over what appeared to be a semantic argument, but it had major political overtones. If environmental sustainability was not emphasised, what was the point of the commission? If "development" and improving standards of living for poor countries were not emphasised, there would be a revolt by the developing country participants.

That dynamic tension has continued to this date and is at the heart of the lack of consensus over climate change abatement policies. The concerns of the commission were more academic and abstract than greenhouse gas targets and quotas but difficult nonetheless. In due course, Nitin Desai produced a definition of sustainable development which has become the accepted standard: "Development that meets the needs of the present without compromising the ability of future generations to meet their own needs."

Significantly, "sustainable development" did not preclude economic growth, even rapid growth, provided that this did not permanently compromise what came to be called "sources" and "sinks": "sources" of clean water, forests and fish stocks; "sinks" to soak up emissions of pollution and waste. Subsequent debate has centred on numbers and practicality, rather than the basic concept that meaningful development has to be sustainable.

There were several areas where the commission, while not original in any fundamental sense, was helpful in promoting awareness of some big new issues. One was species extinction. An Oxford scientist, Norman Myers, who worked with the commission, was able to dramatise the argument with recent estimates that the rate of species loss was much higher than previously estimated. Another was the link between environmental degradation, a scramble for cultivable land and conflict which was then becoming apparent in the Horn of Africa and is now more widely recognised, in Darfur for example. And, despite the big ideological polarisation in the group there was an explicit acknowledgement of the role of markets: environmental taxes or traded permits and the removal of subsidies on energy use or water which artificially stimulate demand for environmentally damaging activities.

But, looked at in a historical perspective, perhaps the biggest contribution which the commission collectively and Ramphal personally made, was to produce the first major international report highlighting the threat of global warming and climate change. An embryonic scientific consensus had formed at a conference in Bellagio in 1985 and through a British scientist based in Sweden, Gordon Goodman, its analysis was fed into the commission's work.

There is little doubt, with hindsight, that the Brundtland Commission had much greater influence than any of the other UN commissions. The Brandt Commission made more initial impact, but few of its policy prescriptions led anywhere and it tended to look back to the intellectual fashions of the 1970s and the centrality of bodies such as UNCTAD. By contrast, Brundtland dealt with, and anticipated, an emerging set of concerns and provided a language and approach for dealing with them. Sonny Ramphal's particular achievement was to ensure that development was at the heart of this new subject matter, and that developing countries' concerns are properly recognised.

The Brundtland Report was launched just before the 1987 CHOGM in Vancouver, and arrived in a context when global environmental concerns were beginning to strike a chord with policymakers. The 1987 Commonwealth summit saw the narrative taken on in an unexpected way.

The head of a new member state, President Gayoom of the Maldives, referred to a recent storm surge which had caused large flood damage in his country of low lying atolls, and asked if there was a connection with the new theory of global warming and sea level rise. I suspect that not all the heads were persuaded that here was a serious issue. For a while Gayoom's contribution was treated a little like the requests of Sir Eric Gairy, former Prime Minister of Grenada, for studies into flying saucers. Ramphal, however, saw the connection with the bigger picture and oversaw the establishment of a Commonwealth Expert Group under the British scientist Martin Holgate.

The study which this group produced in 1989 was arguably the first major inter-governmental report on climate change and sea level rise. The conclusions are not controversial now but, at the time, broke new ground. The group, which included developed and developing country representatives from a wide range of backgrounds, first set out in rigorous, and very qualified terms, the then scientific consensus and the consensus forecast for global warming and sea level rise. It then sought to analyse possible impacts, concentrating in particular on the possible impact of rising sea levels on Guyana, Bangladesh, the Maldives, and a group of Pacific Islands.

These detailed studies were, I believe, the first of their kind, and provided some important impetus to technical work supported by international aid on flood defences. On a broader level the expert group highlighted the way in which climate change would bear down disproportionately on the world's poorest people: more exposed to the risks attendant on rain-fed agriculture; very often in the most marginal and disaster-prone areas; and with few resources to adapt to change. At the same time, the world's poorest people have made the least contribution to global emissions.

The Holgate recommendations consisted, for the most part, of practical steps which the mostly poor and small countries of the Commonwealth could take to improve their own capacity to monitor climate change and sea level rise, and adapt, and contribute to global negotiations on the issue. One important, practical consequence of this work was that it contributed to the establishment of the small states' group, AOSIS (the association of small island developing states) which has been a counterweight to the domination of big energy-producing and energy-using countries in the climate change debate. Sonny Ramphal's Caribbean background, and sensitivity to the special concerns and vulnerability of small states, meant that there was strong political backing for these moves.

Because of Ramphal's work on the Brundtland Commission and the report of the Holgate group, the Commonwealth and he personally were well placed to play a leading, catalytic role in the negotiations on global environmental issues which gathered momentum in the late 1980s and early 1990s. An agreement was reached on limiting emission of gases which damage the ozone layer – the Montreal Protocol – and both Mrs Thatcher and the Kenyan president, Daniel Arap Moi, played an important role in the formative process. The bigger and more complex issues around climate change have taken much longer to reach agreement, but the Intergovernmental Panel on Climate Change, which has taken forward and developed a scientific consensus, was established at this time.

As Ramphal prepared to leave the Secretariat two other initiatives were launched at the 1989 CHOGM in Malaysia, which built on the organisation's growing reputation for topical, pioneering, technically competent work in the environmental field. They came at a time when governments were beginning to think forward to the Rio Earth Summit of 1992, and the Commonwealth summit retreat in Langkawi led to a declaration on the environment.

The President of Guyana offered a million acres of rainforest in his country to set aside as a research project to study the sustainable development of tropical forest. Ramphal promptly set up a planning group under the Indian scientist, M. S. Swaminathan for what became known as the Iwokrama programme. The Secretariat acted as a midwife to an important scientific exercise which has drawn on the resources of Kew, and the many other Commonwealth centres of excellence.

Another piece of work has addressed the issue of disaster insurance, and the limitations of the reinsurance market for vulnerable states. Those in the Caribbean and elsewhere may expect to face more extreme and more frequent hurricanes as a result of climate change. The Secretariat analysis, conducted with the benefit of the expertise of the London reinsurance market, contributed to the establishment of a disaster insurance fund. This strengthens insurance cover for the states most vulnerable to natural disasters.

Sonny Ramphal's involvement was necessarily limited to the less technical aspects of the environmental work of the Secretariat, but he gave important political and intellectual leadership. He never allowed the argument to stray for long into the rather self-indulgent world of many rich world environmentalists who abhor advances in material living standards from the comfort zone of existing affluence, and feel threatened by the aspirations of poor countries to enjoy standards of life long taken for granted in the developed world.

Ramphal's argument was always that poverty is the biggest polluter – because poverty forces those at the margins of existence to act in the interests of short-term survival, even if this means aggravating problems of forest destruction, soil erosion and resource depletion. Sustainability and development are complementary, not in opposition. In a succession of books and speeches, and in his work for the Rockefeller Foundation after leaving the Secretariat, Sonny Ramphal made a continuing contribution to understanding and promoting the concept of sustainable development.

Appendix

SHRIDATH SURENDRANATH RAMPHAL:
a curriculum vitae

Born New Amsterdam, Berbice, Guyana, 3 October 1928

Married – Lois née King

Two daughters, two sons

EDUCATION AND PROFESSIONAL BACKGROUND

Queen's College, Georgetown

Barrister-at-Law, Gray's Inn London, 1951

King's College London, LLM 1952

Gray's Inn, Arden and Atkin Prize, 1952

Harvard University, Guggenheim Fellow, 1962

Queen's Counsel, British Guiana, 1965

Senior Counsel, Guyana, 1966

Honorary Master of the Bench, Gray's Inn, 1981.

Visiting Professor: Exeter University, 1986;
University of Windsor, Canada (Paul Martin Professor)
King's College London, (Law Faculty) 1988
University of Toronto Law School, (Bertha Wilson Professor) 1995
Osgoode Hall Law School, York University, Toronto, 1995

CURRENT ACTIVITIES

Member of Board of Trustees, Rajiv Gandhi Foundation

Chancellor Emeritus, University of the West Indies

Member, Regional Eminent Persons Selection Panel, Anthony N. Sabga Caribbean Awards for Excellence

RECENT ACTIVITIES

Co-Agent and Counsel, Guyana, Guyana-Suriname Maritime Arbitration, 2004-2007

Facilitator, Belize, OAS Mediation Process for Belize-Guatemala Border Dispute, 2000-02

Chancellor, University of the West Indies (UWI), 1989-2003

Chancellor, University of Warwick, UK 1989-2001

Chief Negotiator for the Caribbean on External Economic Relations, 1997-2001

Chairman, Board of Directors, International IDEA – Institute for Democracy and Electoral Assistance, Stockholm, 1995-2001

President, LEAD International (a programme to promote Leadership for Environment and Development), 1991-97

Council Member, International Negotiating Network (INN), Carter Centre, 1991-97

Member of the Board, International Development Research Centre (IDRC), Ottawa, 1990-97

Chairman, Advisory Committee, Future Generations Alliance Foundation, Kyoto, 1995-97

President of the World Conservation Union (IUCN), 1990-93

Special Adviser to the UN Conference on Environment and Development, 1992

Chancellor, University of Guyana, 1988-92

Member of the Earth Council, 19972Secretary-General of the Commonwealth, 1975-90

INTERNATIONAL COMMISSIONS

Member: Independent Commission on International Development Issues – 1980

Independent Commission on Disarmament and Security Issues – 1982

Independent Commission on International Humanitarian Issues – 1988

World Commission on Environment and Development – 1987

South Commission – 1990

Carnegie Commission on Preventing Deadly Conflict – 1994

Co-Chairman: Commission on Global Governance, 1992-2000

Chairman: West Indian Commission, 1990-92

UN Committee on Development Planning, 1984-87

GOVERNMENT OFFICES

Minister of Foreign Affairs and of Justice, Guyana, 1973-75

Minister of Foreign Affairs and Attorney-General, Guyana, 1972-73

Minister of State for External Affairs, Guyana, 1967-72

Attorney-General, Guyana, 1965-73

Assistant Attorney-General, West Indies, 1961-62

Solicitor-General, British Guiana, 1959-61

First Legal Draftsman, West Indies, 1958-59

Legal positions in British Guiana, 1953-58

Vice-President, UN General Assembly, 1968 & 1973

HONOURS AND AWARDS

National

Companion of the Order of St Michael and St George (CMG), 1966 (UK/British Guiana)

Knight Bachelor (Kt), 1970 (UK/Guyana)

Order of the Republic, 1973 (Arab Republic of Egypt)
Grand Cross, Order of the Sun 1974 (Peru)
Grand Cross, Order of Merit 1974 (Ecuador)
Companion of the Order of Australia, 1982 (Australia)
Order of Excellence (OE), 1983 (Guyana)
Order of Nishaan Izzuddeen 1989 (Maldives)
Knight Grand Cross of the Order of St Michael and St George (GCMG) 1990 (UK)
Order of New Zealand (OZ) 1990 (New Zealand)
Grand Commander of the Order of the Niger (GCON) 1990 (Nigeria)
Grand Commander of the Order of the Companion of Freedom 1990 (Zambia)
Nishan-e-Quaid-i-Azam 1990 (Pakistan)
Order of Merit (OM) 1990 (Jamaica)
Order of the Caribbean Community (OCC) 1991
Commander of the Order of the Golden Ark (Netherlands) 1994
Medal of Friendship (Cuba) 2001
Indira Gandhi Prize for Peace, Disarmament & Development (India) 2002
Pravasi Bharatiya Samman Award, 2003
Order of Belize, 2003
Order of the Supreme Companions of O.R.Tambo -Gold (South Africa) 2007

Academic

Fellow, King's College London, 1975
Fellow, London School of Economics, 1979
Fellow, Magdalen College, Oxford, 1982
Hon. LLD: Panjab, India 1975; Southampton, 1976; St Francis Xavier, Canada, 1978;
    Univ. of West Indies, 1978; Aberdeen, 1979; Cape Coast, Ghana, 1980;
    London, 1981; Benin, 1982; Hull, 1983; Yale, 1985; Cambridge, 1985;
    Warwick, 1988; York, Canada, 1988; Malta, 1989; Otago, 1990; Staffordshire 1993
Hon DUniv.: Surrey, 1979; Essex 1980
Hon DHL: Simmons College, USA, 1982; Duke, USA, 1985
Hon DCL: Oxford 1982; East Anglia 1983; Durham 1985
Hon DLitt: Bradford, 1985; Indira Gandhi National Open University, 1989
Hon DSc: Cranfield Institute of Technology, 1987
International Education Award, Richmond College, London, 1988
Companionship of de Montfort University, UK 1991

Societies and Institutes

Fellow, Royal Society of Arts London, 1981
Albert Medal, Royal Society of Arts, 1988
Rene Dubos Environment Award, 1993
Aurelio Peccei Award, 1995

PUBLICATIONS

One World to Share: Selected Speeches of the Commonwealth Secretary-General 1975–79 (Hutchinson Benham, London, 1979)

Nkrumah and the Eighties (Kwame Nkrumah Memorial Lectures, 1980; Third World Foundation Monograph, London, 1980)

Sovereignty or Solidarity (Thomas Callander Memorial Lectures; University of Aberdeen, 1981)

Challenges for the Lawyer in our Interdependent World (The Cambridge Lectures: Butterworths, 1983)

'Some in Light and Some in Darkness': the Long Shadow of Slavery (Third World Foundation Monograph, London, 1983)

The Trampling of the Grass (Inaugural Silver Jubilee Lecture of the Economic Commission for Arica: UNECA, 1985

The End of the Beginning: Apartheid in Crisis (Address to the International Defence and Aid fund for Southern Africa); 1985

Roots and Reminders (Address to the Royal Commonwealth Society of India, New Delhi; 1986)

For the South: A Time to Think (Paper for South-South II, Kuala Lumpur: 1986)

Making Human Society A Civilised State (11th Corbishley Memorial Lecture, Royal Society of Arts, London) 1987

'Life is One and the World is One': Reflections on Peace (1987 Indira Gandhi Memorial Lecture, published by the Association of Indian Diplomats, New Delhi, 1987)

The South African Crisis: Why the Bell of Aparthied Tolls for Everyone (third ISIS World Affairs Lecture, Kuala Lumpur; 1988)

Compulsions of Excellence: Shadows and Reality (Address on Installation as Chancellor of the University of Guyana, Turkeyne: 1988

Inseparable Humanity: An Anthology of Reflections of Shridath Ramphal, edited by Ron Sanders (Hansib, London, 1988)

The Black must be Discharged (Kapila Memorial Lecture, Grays Inn, London) 1988

A Heritage of Oneness (Inaugural Lecture in The Genesis of a Nation Series, Guyana) 1988

Endangered Earth: Inaugural Address of the Cambridge Lectures on Environment and Development, 1989.

Vivat, Floreat, Crescat (Address at the 40th Anniversary Convocation of the University of the West Indies, Jamaica, 1989

An End to Otherness: Commemorative Addresses by the Commonwealth Secretary-General (Commonwealth Secretariat, London, 1990)

Keeping the Faith: From Kingston to Kuala Lumpur and Beyond (a Valedictory Address, London: 1990)

Our Country, The Planet: Forging a Partnership for Survival. (Lime Tree, London, and Island Press, Washington DC, 1992)

Global Governance and New Dimensions of Human Security (Sir John Crawford Memorial Lecture, Washington DC, 1995)

Global Governance (The Second Global Security Lecture, Oxford) 1995

West Indian Space in the 21st Centrury (Address in the West Indian Lectures, Kingston:1998)

No Island is an Island (Warwick University, Caribbean Studies, 2000)

Governance and the New Imperium (Address to the Mona Academic Conference, 'Governance in the age of Globalisation, UWI, Kingston: 2002)

Can the Rule of Law in the Commonwealth be Secure in a Lawless World? (Address to the Commonwealth Law Conference, London; 2005)

Index